W9-CTG-534

style by nature

beautify your home with nature's colors and textures

Better Homes and Gardens® Books
Des Moines, Iowa

Better Homes and Gardens₀ Books
An imprint of Meredith₀ Books

STYLE BY NATURE
Writer and Stylist: Rebecca Jerdee
Editor: Vicki L. Ingham
Senior Associate Design Director: Sundie Ruppert, Studio G Design
Copy Chief: Terri Fredrickson
Copy and Production Editor: Victoria Forlini
Editorial Operations Manager: Karen Schirm
Managers, Book Production: Pam Kvitne, Marjorie J. Schenkelberg, Rick von Holdt
Contributing Copy Editor: Kim Catanzarite
Contributing Proofreaders: Beth Lastine, Nancy Ruhling, Willa Speiser
Contributing Photographers: Kim Cornelison, Scott Little, William Stites
Indexer: Stephanie J. Reymann
Electronic Production Coordinator: Paula Forest
Editorial and Design Assistants: Kaye Chabot, Karen McFadden, Mary Lee Gavin

Meredith₀ Books
Editor in Chief: Linda Raglan Cunningham
Design Director: Matt Strelecki
Executive Editor, Home Decorating and Design: Denise L. Caringer

Publisher: James D. Blume
Executive Director, Marketing: Jeffrey Myers
Executive Director, New Business Development: Todd M. Davis
Executive Director, Sales: Ken Zagor
Director, Operations: George A. Susral
Director, Production: Douglas M. Johnston
Business Director: Jim Leonard

Vice President and General Manager: Douglas J. Guendel

Better Homes and Gardens₀ Magazine
Vice President/Editor in Chief: Karol DeWulf Nickell
Senior Deputy Editor, Home Design: Oma Blaise Ford

Meredith Publishing Group
President, Publishing Group: Stephen M. Lacy
Vice President-Publishing Director: Bob Mate

Meredith Corporation
Chairman and Chief Executive Officer: William T. Kerr

In Memoriam: E. T. Meredith III (1933–2003)

Copyright © 2003 by Meredith Corporation, Des Moines, Iowa. First Edition.
All rights reserved. Printed in the United States of America.
Library of Congress Control Number: 2003103309
ISBN: 0-696-21460-1

All of us at Better Homes and Gardens₀ Books are dedicated to providing you with information and ideas to enhance your home. We welcome your comments and suggestions. Write to us at: Better Homes and Gardens Books, Home Decorating and Design Editorial Department, 1716 Locust St., Des Moines, IA 50309-3023.

If you would like to purchase any of our home decorating and design, cooking, crafts, gardening, or home improvement books, check wherever quality books are sold. Or visit us at: bhgbooks.com

"The Bare Tree" from *The Niche Narrows: New and Selected Poems* (Talisman House) by Samuel Menashe reprinted by permission.
Excerpt from "Prose #57" from *Gitanjali* by Rabindranath Tagore (New York: Scribner Poetry, 1997). Used by permission of Scribner, an imprint of Simon & Schuster Adult Publishing Group.
"Bouquet" from *Collected Poems* (1976) by Robert Francis reprinted by permission of The University of Massachusetts Press.

6 introduction
one room four ways

16 quiz
what's your style?

188 resources
bringing your natural style home

192 index
find what you're looking for

18 spring
s t y l e

IF YOU'RE A ROMANTIC SPIRIT

drawn to the pale and pretty palette of

tender buds and delicate flowers, this may

be your style. Spring style uses soft colors

to enlarge spaces with a feeling of light and

airy openness, and floral themes blossom on

fabrics, furnishings, and accessories. Learn

to breathe sweet life into your living room,

dining room, and bedrooms using the colors,

patterns, and motifs of awakening nature.

54 summer
s t y l e

BOUNDARIES BLUR BETWEEN INDOORS

and out with summer style. Choose from

two personalities: an extrovert who loves

the joy of bold, saturated colors or a quiet

introvert who finds refreshment in summer-

white minimalism. In either case, you'll rely

on large-scale furnishings and accessories

to create uncluttered spaces. Discover how

to combine color and pattern, where to find

inspiration, and how to bring lighthearted

whimsy to your rooms.

90 autumn
s t y l e

IF YOU'RE A COLLECTOR who loves to be surrounded by your favorite things, autumn may be your style. Accessories come first, backgrounds last for this decorating personality. Layered displays of beloved objects on shelves, mantels, and tables create a snug sense of security that's echoed by furniture arrangements, rustic textures, and rich dark colors. Study this chapter for ways to bring cozy warmth to your nest.

126 winter
s t y l e

IF YOU'RE DESPERATELY SEEKING SERENITY, look to winter for inspiration. Winter-style personalities rely on well-edited collections and minimal pattern to create a soothing environment. This style uses high contrasts—bare-bones architecture softened by rounded furniture shapes, smooth surfaces warmed by touchable textiles, quiet neutrals enlivened by a jolt of color—to create an environment that calms and nourishes you. Explore this chapter for easy ideas to bring simplicity and tranquillity to your rooms.

162 project
p r i m e r

24 EASY WINDOW TREATMENTS

Dress your windows to suit your natural style. Six ideas for each season include instructions for framed panels, window-frame embellishments, no-sew and simple-to-sew curtains and shades, upholstered bifold doors that serve as shutters, and ideas for customizing ready-mades.

SPRING-STYLE

one touch of nature makes the whole world kin

William Shakespeare

You know it well: the compelling urge to create a home. It's second nature. Like a bird gathering bits and pieces to fashion a warm nest, you select attractive items from the world around you and weave them into a place of contentment called home. This is a book about you. It's about decorating by way of your instincts and feelings, about creating your home with an inherent sense of what's right. It's about gathering bits and pieces from nature and bringing them inside to make your home more beautiful and comfortable. More specifically, this book is about discovering your natural decorating style in light of your favorite season and using the season's style as your decorating guide. In this chapter, you'll find clues to your natural style simply by looking at a few photographs and taking a decorating quiz. Are you a spring-, summer-, autumn-, or winter-style nest builder? A blend of two or more? To find out, begin the style-by-nature tour by turning the next few pages and seeing how a single room is interpreted in four seasonal styles. After you've noted which one appeals to you most, turn to page 16 for more clues to your inborn nest-building ways.

Observe spring to bring it to bloom in a room. Ask yourself: Is it soft rain on a windowpane that inspires me to hang sheer panels as curtains? Do tulips and lilacs generate the desire for fabric choices in similar pictorial patterns? Does the sunlight draw me toward the windows and suggest that I sit nearby to take in its warmth? Decorating clues emerge wherever you choose to see them; it's only a matter of giving your observations permission to decorate.

signs of spring

Still cool from winter's snow cover, nature's newborn colors and textures slip into a waiting world. Pale and citrusy, spring's garden colors arrive fresh and light. Likewise the season's newly formed textures are smooth as silk sheets, soft as lamb's wool, translucent as lace curtains, and delicate as the embroidery on a baby's bonnet.

The first room of this one-room-four-ways demonstration, *opposite,* is only one example of how to translate spring's inspirations into room-furnishing materials. If you're drawn to the spring style, your translation very well might be different. In any case, memories and experiences of spring play into this selection of decorating elements. The overall plan is simple: white sheer curtains and window shades create a light and airy backdrop, like a misty morning in spring. Light wood floors, muslin-covered furniture, and an ivory slipcover on the sofa keep the room's palette pale. This allows flowery color accents to come from floral fabrics on pillows and a chair, garden-path rugs, and touches of fresh green in live plants and apples. How does the room make you feel? Turn the page and compare it to summer's style.

What's your first reaction to this room? (First impressions are the most telling.) Could an exuberant hibiscus coax you into bringing home a giant floral print for a room screen, or do you know you'd soon grow weary of its presence? Do white clouds inspire you to buy soft, puffy sofa cushions covered in washable canvas slipcovers? Do you gravitate toward saturated colors? If you ask yourself questions like these, your natural style will reveal itself. It's all within your heart.

style profile
summer signals

Same room, same sofa, same chair. What has changed are the colors and patterns, not to mention the mood. Comfortable in this room? Thrilled? Shocked? When you compare the spring-style room (page 8) to the summer version here, you see color's ability to commandeer a room's mood. A little vibrant color goes a long way, and exuberant pattern takes over. No doubt the energetic floral panel room screen first grabbed your attention, leaping into the room like an excited puppy. Then you picked up on the zany, dotted rug and orange accent pillows. To balance the powers of color, nature demonstrates proportion. It counters small dollops of color with great doses of white—like colorful shells scattered across a wide beach of powdery-white sand. This room takes a lesson from nature and counters the bold brights with a relaxing white background and overall framework of white. Note how you feel about this setting. Then turn the page to compare spring and summer to autumn's way with decorating.

Look for clues in nature to bring harmony and balance home. Autumn is an especially good source for the warm neutrals that provide palpable comforts in a room. When leaves fall from the trees, gather them up and fan them out in your hands to see how the colors glow against each other. One does not outdo another. Take them with you to find similar colors at paint or fabric stores, and gather a collection of colors, patterns, and textures for future reference. Note the myriad leaf patterns artists have interpreted in decorative fabrics.

autumn gestures

Use different strokes of color, pattern, and texture like these, and you can recapture memories of the earth rolling up its colorful carpet and turning inward. As the sun distances itself, natural colors fade and rich textures remain. Feeling comfortable? Warm and calm? Sad? Autumn is the going-home part of nature that spawns a color palette that's easy on the eyes and easy to bring inside. A bundle of dried hydrangeas directed the natural, autumn-style color scheme for this room. Equal amounts of green, tan, and rust teach us that low-key colors make great neighbors. A leaf-patterned runner pulls everything together. Turn the page to see what winter offers.

Do the elegant, barely there patterns of frost spun across your window make you wish for permanently frosted windows? Do you love the sight of bare trees in a snowy wood and wonder how you could bring the high-contrast look inside? If so, note the dark and light colors you see and the subtle textures that stand out. Keep them in mind as you turn the pages of wallcovering books in search of subtle wintry patterns or when you visit fabric stores to buy upholstery fabrics to make pillows for your home.

traces of winter

Same room, same seating, but this time the interpretation is one of wintery freshness. How does the room make you feel? Cold enough to imagine your breath in the air? Calm and serene? Perhaps you're intrigued by the idea of bringing winter's cool style inside. Depending on how you interpret it in materials, winter's style may not look much different from spring's. After all, winter and spring resemble each other in their pale and fragile looks. Merged in slumber, winter dreams of spring, and from winter spring emerges. Compare this room to spring's room on page 8 to discern the similarities and differences. Then take the quiz on page 16.

What's your style?

TAKE THIS QUIZ to see which season is most likely to inspire your decorating. If none of the answers appeals to you, select the closest one. When you've finished, transfer your answers to the scoring columns on the next page, then analyze the results to discover your natural decorating style.

1 The colors you love to live with are:
a. Pastel
b. Bright
c. Golds, oranges, and browns
d. Grays, blacks, and whites

2 Your sofa needs livening up, so you choose:
a. Pillows in a mix of floral fabrics
b. One or two dot or stripe pillows
c. Big, comfortable pillows in brown tones
d. One or two exquisite handcrafted pillows

3 Out of four invitations, you choose to attend:
a. A garden show
b. A street fair celebration
c. An estate sale at an 1896 mansion
d. A gallery exhibiting Japanese pottery

4 For a dinner party, you dress the table with:
a. Delicate, hand-painted china
b. Flamboyant colors
c. Family china
d. Glass plates on dark metal chargers

5 For slipcovers in your living room, you choose:
a. Canvas for the sofa, floral prints for chairs
b. Cotton duck for the sofa, denim for chairs
c. Corduroy for the sofa, chenille for chairs
d. Leather for the sofa, suede for chairs

6 For your living room windows, you choose:
a. Sheers or lace panels
b. Plantation shutters
c. Bamboo blinds and plaid side panels
d. Frosted glass or no coverings

7 What mood do you want your home to convey?
a. Romantic and relaxed
b. Carefree and fun
c. Warm and hospitable
d. Serene and subtle

8 On weekends, you're likely to wear:
a. Slacks and a voile blouse
b. Jeans and a white T-shirt
c. Jeans and a buffalo-check shirt
d. Khakis and a white silk shirt

9 If you bought a new bed, it would be:
a. A pine frame and a garden-gate headboard
b. A mattress and springs on a metal frame
c. A poster bed
d. An upholstered platform bed

10 You're off on that long-awaited vacation to:
a. Visit Kew Gardens in London
b. Cruise the ocean
c. Visit Napa Valley for a wine-tasting tour
d. Ski in Colorado

11 You prefer to cover your floors with:
a. Light-colored hardwood
b. Beach mats or sisal over terrazzo
c. Wall-to-wall carpet
d. Slate or ceramic tile

12 Your dream house is:
a. A Victorian "painted lady"
b. A tiny apartment on the French Riviera
c. A log home with windows to nature
d. A gallery-style loft with skylights

13 You never miss your favorite TV "home" show:
a. Rachel Ashwell
b. Trading Spaces
c. Christopher Lowell
d. House Beautiful

14 For you, the perfect reading chair is:
a. A down-filled chair covered in chenille
b. A bamboo chair with squishy cushions
c. An antique Chippendale wing chair
d. A steel-and-leather Le Corbusier chaise

15 You're most excited about nature when:
a. Daffodils and tulips pop up
b. Parks and beaches open
c. Turning leaves rustle in the wind
d. Pure, white snow expands the landscape

16 The room in this chapter you liked best is:
a. Signs of spring
b. Summer signals
c. Autumn gestures
d. Traces of winter

17 For seating around an antique farm table, you:
a. Paint mismatched chairs cottage white
b. Surround it with white patio chairs
c. Search for chairs of the same vintage
d. Pull up postmodern chairs

18 For mantelpiece art, you choose:
a. An arrangement of fragile antique plates
b. A Matisse poster
c. The crazy quilt you found at a garage sale
d. An African kuba cloth framed in black

SCORING After you've circled "a," "b," "c," or "d" for each question, transfer your answers to the appropriate columns below. Then total each column at the bottom. The column with the highest score indicates the season that aligns best with the nature side of you.

COLUMN 1	COLUMN 2	COLUMN 3	COLUMN 4
1. a	1. b	1. c	1. d
2. a	2. b	2. c	2. d
3. a	3. b	3. c	3. d
4. a	4. b	4. c	4. d
5. a	5. b	5. c	5. d
6. a	6. b	6. c	6. d
7. a	7. b	7. c	7. d
8. a	8. b	8. c	8. d
9. a	9. b	9. c	9. d
10. a	10. b	10. c	10. d
11. a	11. b	11. c	11. d
12. a	12. b	12. c	12. d
13. a	13. b	13. c	13. d
14. a	14. b	14. c	14. d
15. a	15. b	15. c	15. d
16. a	16. b	16. c	16. d
17. a	17. b	17. c	17. d
18. a	18. b	18. c	18. d
TOTAL	TOTAL	TOTAL	TOTAL

ANALYZING THE RESULTS Now you can use your answers to decide which nature style describes you best. Are you a spring spirit, a summer sprite, an autumn fan, or a winter soul? Or, are you a blend of one or two seasons? No matter which architecture or furniture style you prefer—romantic, cottage, 18th century, Art Deco, modern—your natural style fits in with what you already have.

spring style If most of your answers were in Column 1, spring's open and airy style is your heart's desire. You may like a touch of formality, a gracious melding of timeless, classic furnishings. Or, you may be romantically relaxed in a blend of soft pastels and floral patterns. The chapter on spring style begins on page 18.

summer style If the majority of your answers landed in Column 2, your attitude toward decorating style walks on the bright and happy side. You like things simple and carefree, like a swing in the hammock or a picnic on the beach. Your home's primary request: Put your feet up and enjoy. Turn to page 54 to read more about decorating with summer's inspirations.

autumn style If most of your answers were in Column 3, you like a casual decorating style. You choose furnishings with relaxed comfort in mind, and you prefer unfussy seating with easy-care fabrics in earthy or neutral colors. Seating is arranged in informal groupings for easy con-

versation. You'll feel at home in the autumn-style chapter that begins on page 90.

winter style If the majority of your answers fell in Column 4, you like. an elegantly simple look inspired by your interests in art and design. You carefully edit furnishings and accessories, choosing each element for its distinctive lines. Even color is often kept to a minimum, with hues drawn from the neutrals—especially black, white, and gray—often punched up with a brilliant accent color. Check out the winter-style chapter on page 126.

seasonal mix If your answers are spread over the four seasons, you're confident about what you love and want to combine the best from each style. Chances are your answers lean at least slightly toward one category. The key is to understand and heed your main attitude toward furnishing your home so you can combine disparate elements into a harmonious whole. For instance, if you lean toward romantic springtime ruffles but also love winter's simplicity, you might team ivory-colored ruffled pillow shams with a contemporary stainless-steel bed frame. Throughout this book, you'll find examples of split-season decorating that work.

Your exciting, new challenge is to create beautiful, comfortable rooms that draw on the best resource of all—your natural style.

And the spring

arose on the
garden fair,
Like the spirit of love felt everywhere;

And each flower and herb on Earth's dark breast
Rose from the dreams of its wintry rest.

From "The Sensitive Plant" by Percy Bysshe Shelley

When spring flutters like a pale blue ribbon in the lilac-scented breeze, it unfurls a delicate palette of colors, patterns, and textures that inspires everything from spring fever to freshening the interior of your home. As new and promising as daybreak, spring's tender shoots, mountain laurels, luxurious peonies, and rose-petal delights form a shy, emerging parade of decorating cues that, when pulled together, forms a cohesive formula for interior design. You'll find spring's special style in this chapter.

spring style

Like a breath of fresh air through sheer curtains, spring's fanciful style comes inside by way of Eden's garden. The newest part of the natural year, spring overflows with decorating cues that are easy to imitate: a pale and pretty palette of colors, soft textures, fragile newborn flowers, shoots of lime greens, and sunlight that's just the right temperature. To embrace spring style, think of your interior as a garden. Face furnishings outward to the light, place them near windows that have inspiring natural views, and gather them around openings that connect to whatever outdoor living spaces you possess. A soft white spring-style interior invites you inside but also beckons you through breezy doorways to secret gardens beyond. Here, away from the business of the day, you can relax, unwind, and quietly connect with the things that really matter. In this chapter, see how you can bring spring's spirit to life inside your house, no matter what your home's style of architecture or furnishings. If you're a spring-style person, you'll find that these decorating cues work for you year-round.

spring-style home

Ivory furnishings step quietly into the background,

providing comfortable display spaces for beloved floral

prints and dishware. Even the French doors' cream-

colored lace panels offer a place for a posy.

setting up

It's easy to produce spring's open and airy style if you begin with a white-box suburban space, a city apartment with white walls, or an older home that has been completely whitewashed inside. If you have to paint walls and woodwork, choose an ivory color that warms the interior while keeping it light and simple. A single color used throughout the house results in rooms that flow easily one into the next. When you choose the furniture (building blocks of the rooms), pick antique-white tables and storage pieces, and creamy-white slipcovered sofas and chairs. For furnishing outdoor spaces, assemble weather-worthy wicker in intimate groups.

accessorizing

The most enjoyable part of putting together this look is finding the right accessories. In its most energized state, spring style bursts forth in bloom, which is wonderful considering there's no end to the pretty floral items you can gather from all kinds of boutiques and stores. Painted dishes and artwork, printed fabrics, silk flowers, dainty tiles and bottles, laces and garden flowers are just the beginning. Don't resist the urge to collect. Spring style encourages you to fill your cupboards with an abundance of practical pretties and overflow your seating pieces with touchable, inviting pillows that cushion and comfort. Always remember: A good house is never finished. Continue to make changes for the way you live and let your rooms evolve.

LEFT

Dining chair slipcovers, assembled from chenille bedspreads and a floral cotton print, bring more than simple comfort to the table. The texture of chenille, usually reserved for the bedroom, is an unexpected idea and a pleasure to touch.

OPPOSITE

Morning tea tastes best outside when the weather allows. The screen porch extends the useful space of this house, connecting it to nature and the chance to enjoy the scents, sights, and sounds of the outdoors.

RIGHT

Cozy and comforting, a luxurious

bedroom getaway means piles

of pretty pillows and coverlets.

Here an antique door separates

the bedroom from the rest of the

house; French doors on the other

side of the room provide an

escape to the screen porch.

OPPOSITE

Love is in the details. Tender

flowers and delicate accessories

settle onto the ledge of a

between-the-studs niche.

mirror magic

To expand the spring-garden feeling of your home, use panes of glass and mirrors to lighten the interiors. For example, a mirror laid against the back of a dining room hutch (see page 23) adds glittering light. It also appears to double the number of items and lets you enjoy a view of the backs as well as the fronts of beloved objects. Another idea: Include a large mirror in your living room to add glamour. In spring style, each room deserves the glint of chandelier crystals and jewelry-like surfaces that reflect light and dazzle the eye.

spring-style colors

Color courage is easy to find with the spring-style palette because pale colors are so compatible. These schemes suggest three ways to select a personal palette from the field of choices, *right*.

ONE-COLOR-PLUS-WHITE SCHEME. Soft or creamy whites are the backbone of spring-style colors because they're present in all pastel hues. For a super-simple, light-and-airy color scheme, choose one favorite color to use with a warm-toned ivory white.

ANALOGOUS COLOR SCHEME. Neighboring, or analogous, colors are closely related and flow naturally one to another without abrupt interruption. For this scheme, choose your favorite pastel from the paint rack at the paint store. This will be your dominant or main color. Then select additional colors from the neighboring strips on either side of your dominant color.

COMPLEMENTARY COLOR SCHEME. Opposites on the color wheel attract, and in the pastel world of spring style, opposing colors are easy to live with because they're not intense. Natural spring-style complements include pinks combined with pale greens, lavenders with yellows, or pale blues with peach tones.

lilac and white

lavender, sky blue, and mint

lemon yellow and hyacinth

textures and patterns

Pretty patterns and delectable textures are key to a lively and varied spring-style color scheme. They bring pale color schemes to life with inviting sheers, soft chenilles, rose-petal delicacies, and floral fantasies. One touch of embroidery, a bit of lace or sheer organza, and the room awakens memories of the scent of a lilac bush, the softness of daybreak, or the crisp snap of a green apple between your teeth. When choosing a variety of patterns and textures, use care. After all, if you recognize spring style in your decorating habits, you're a discriminating sort. The first rule: Choose printed patterns that carry a base color of soft white (note the examples, *opposite*). Avoid fabrics and wallcoverings with undertones of beige or tan, which tend to cut back the freshness of spring-style color schemes. Second, choose prints of various sizes and designs, avoiding too many florals. If you must have an abundance of florals, vary the sizes of the flower images and maintain the same color scheme in all. Then toss in a plaid, a check, or a dot for contrast. Finally, include one-color fabrics with dimensional textures for that invitation to touch.

Self-professed "hopeless romantics" are a natural fit for the cozy-cottage genre of decorating. If you qualify as a spring-style hopeless romantic, you're attracted to pretty (not necessarily fancy) things that bring life to small, intimate spaces. At the same time, you're not completely ruled by your heart; you also choose furnishings for their practicality as well as for their charm.

Color is the secret ingredient that successfully links a diverse collection of favorite pieces. Neutral ivory walls and furniture with creamy-white slipcovers blend together as a quiet backdrop that gives you opportunities for showing off the objects of your affections. Large neutral elements showcase special pieces rather than compete with them. In this room, an elegant rug tops a bland beige carpet, artwork slips into nooks, and fresh flowers breathe life into the space.

spring-style
living

are you a spring spirit?

If you're one of those spring-style spirits who is deeply affected by sunshine, you need open, airy spaces with lots of windows that let in the light and blur the boundaries between indoors and out. Dark and cozy rooms aren't for you—they're too suffocating. You opt for carpetless, light-colored floors softened by area rugs that define living spaces. You paint and paper walls in pale colors that reflect light, so even when it's gray outside, you feel sunny and happy inside. No matter what your furniture style—cottage, country, contemporary, or classic—you can apply nature's color, pattern, and texture cues to get the mood you desire. Turn the pages to see ways to infuse rooms with the spring look using a variety of furniture styles.

Painted walls are the quickest way to develop spring style in a contemporary setting.

OPPOSITE

Nature's presence makes an impression in this sunroom. Garden furniture, flower-print fabrics, and a sisal rug erase the line between the inside and out. Metal tables and chandeliers lean toward a more classical take on spring style.

growing open spaces

You don't have to live in a palace to reap the benefits of large-space living. Spring style has a natural tendency toward space stretching and room expansion by virtue of its lighthearted elements. To make your rooms live big, hang window treatments from the highest possible point on the wall to let the fabric flow freely and make the room stand up to its full height. Include built-ins that take up almost no floor space and provide plenty of storage. Add glaze to wall paint to reflect the light. If possible, open rooms to each other with pass-throughs and French doors that make them feel bigger. Define spaces subtly, choosing similar wall colors and flooring throughout the house. Paint all woodwork the same color so one room flows easily into the next.

style points

The heart of spring-style decorating hinges on the desire to blur boundaries between nature and the hard-edged walls and doors of a house. The marriage of nature's irregular forms and the geometry of architecture results in a sweet compromise: Built structures are softened and warmed by natural light and the proverbial Garden of Eden comes inside. The spring-style points shown here are just a few ways to soften the lines of your home.

1 Grow grass indoors by seeding a liner that fits inside a garden tray. 2 Decorate with transparent furniture and accessories for a see-through, airy look. 3 Choose fabrics with white backgrounds so you can freely mix spring-style colors and patterns. 4 Keep sidelights uncovered to invite the sunlight inside. 5 Use your broken china to create mosaics on watering cans and old silver-plated teapots. Then fill them with flowers.

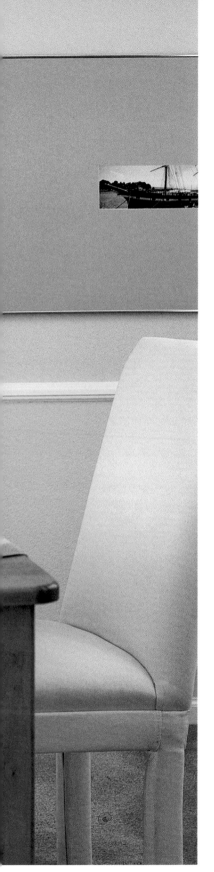

Sometimes a natural object ushers you rapidly through the door of decorating inspiration. A delicate pink-and-white-striped shell and seafaring images, shot with a wide-angle panoramic lens, gave rise to this contemporary spring-style dining room. The vacation snapshots, treated like fine art, are framed in wide mats of whisper-soft colors and hung at diners' eye level. The horizontal line of pictures grounds the space with a sense of low-lying serenity; the wall, painted a foamy green below the chair rail and a misty lavender above it, mimics the colors of sea and sky.

spring-style dining

A vertically striped wallcovering and lumberyard moldings create a do-it-yourself plate rack that sets the color scheme for this fresh-as-a-daisy kitchen scene. The moldings are attached to the wall over the panel of wallpaper, offering decorative storage and display shelves for plates and other items, such as a crowd of garden hydrangeas sporting various shades of spring green.

One flower at a time, please
however small the face

Two flowers are one flower
too many, a distraction.

Three flowers in a vase
begin to be a little noisy.

Like cocktail conversation,
everybody talking.

A crowd of flowers is a
crowd of flatterers (forgive me)

One flower at a time,
I want to hear what it is
saying.

"Bouquets" by Robert Francis

two sides to your nature

You may find that your decorating tendencies lean toward two seasons—for instance, spring and autumn. If so, it's possible to come up with a color and pattern compromise that pleases both sides. This dining room is a perfect example of split-season decorating. Like a picnic table set under the trees in a country orchard, this room evokes the feeling of dining al fresco on a spring morning or late afternoon in autumn.

To satisfy two sides of your nature at the same time, choose two or three colors found on both of nature's palettes. For example, the yellows and greens of this dining room occupy both spring and autumn palettes—with slight differences. (See pages 28–29 and pages 100–101.) The greens of autumn's palette are deeper and warmer than spring's citrus and mint; yellows are richer and creamier than the water-thin yellows of spring. In this room, white trim keeps the scheme as light and fresh as spring, but the presence of creamy tans and browns counters with an autumnal mood. Autumn-style textures are generally coarser than spring's fine, delicate surfaces. Choose a few of each; the contrast of the rough with the refined is always pleasing. When it comes to pattern, go either geometric or floral, or combine mostly geometrics with a single floral print as an accent fabric in the room.

1

2

style points

If you qualify as a spring-style personality, you spell delicacy with a capital "D," and your penchant for fine china

and tiny painted flowers takes you into a special decorative realm. Ever on the hunt for Delicate, you stroll through

antiques shops, fine furniture stores, and flower markets—always with the hope of finding something wonderful

to take home. Here are some ways to turn secondhand objects into fresh and dainty accessories that speak of your

spring-style ways.

1 Charm party guests with pansy blooms slipped between a glass charger and a glass plate. 2 Be sentimental. Use your mother's broken china to create a mosaic on a footstool. 3 To give a worn-out chair new life, insert a box where the cane seat used to be. Then fill the box with bedding plants. 4 To express your romantic side, double up on old-fashioned roses. 5 Bring a garden urn indoors to provide a graceful table base.

Spring-style decorators know the value of sleeping on comfortable fabrics, no matter what the style. You're partial to pale colors, plain or printed patterns, and the softest of textures. In this bedroom, window sheers and a striped wallcovering make an airy, clean-lined backdrop for the bed, which is made from two ends of a baby's crib fastened to the head of a king-size bed frame. Cotton bedding, in plain and simple patterns, exemplifies the spirit of those who love to sleep light.

spring-style
sleeping

Ahhh, the luxuries of white. It comes in a variety of colors and textures that add up to glorious sink-in comforts. To assemble a luxury sleeping suite of the spring-style sort, explore ivory in its many textures: soft chenilles, swiss dots, seersucker stripes, sheer organzas, and lace. When you have all the core furniture and bedding pieces in place, give the room a visual kiss with patterned pillow fabrics featuring pink, violet, citrus green, or yellow on an ivory background.

A deep, strong shade taken from the pillow pattern becomes the dominant color of this otherwise pale pink-and-ivory color scheme, enriching the room for the cost of a can of paint. This simple and natural bedroom decor works if you're torn between a love for the light-and-airy softness of spring's style and the cozy depths of a slumberous winter. Place a pillow on a metal garden chair to soften it for use in a bedroom.

style points

It's an indisputable fact: You love flowers. Not only do they inspire you, they also beg you to make them part of

your decorating scenarios. So be it. The best part of an unabashed love affair with flowers is their abundance. You

can plant bulbs or seeds to grow garden blooms yourself, frequent a florist for the luxury of cut flowers, or shop

for delicate fabrics and china to your heart's desire.

1 Go ahead, be extravagant. Bring flowers with breakfast in bed.
2 To successfully mix floral fabrics, choose large, medium, and miniature
patterns in the same color palette. **3** Sew your delicate sensibilities into a
textural pillow with a blossoming center. **4** Add sparkle with a mirror; it
will reflect and double the number of blooms you set in front of it.

...the sky opens,
the wind runs wild,
laughter passes
over the earth...

Mirth spreads from leaf to leaf,
my darling, and gladness
without measure.

The heaven's river has drowned its
banks and the flood of joy is abroad.

From "Prose #57" by Rabindranath Tagore

While other schemes simply invite nature inside the house, summer style likes to meet nature outside. It loves to live in shady nooks, wade in cool waters, and splash about in daring colors. Home is simple, uncluttered, and kicked back. Furnishings are easygoing and lighthearted; some pieces move from indoors to out on a whim. Summer-house types keep their eyes on windows, ever conscious of the promising blue vistas just beyond the red hibiscus in the garden.

summer style

In summer's sunny Garden of Eden, everything is in full bloom and raring to go. Flowers express themselves in brilliant colors; singing birds dive among lush, green branches. Overhead, the blue sky puffs up with billowy white clouds, and the whole world seems to have gone mad with happiness. The slam of a screen door takes you there in an instant. Remember pool passes, flashlight tag, and fireflies caught in a jelly jar? Summer style, simply put, is a revolving door that happily brings the outdoors in to you, then just as happily takes you outside again.

You can let nature's summer style slip through your doors in a variety of ways. One way is quiet, featuring a mood of spare simplicity, relaxation, and a less-is-more type of minimalism. The decorating schemes *opposite* and on the following pages illustrate this approach. Natural wood tones provide virtually the only color in the rooms, and white walls and upholstery frame them. If quiet minimalism isn't what you have in mind, however, summer style comes in other colors too. For a summer attitude filled with the energy and zest of giant sunflowers and zinnias in a garden, color your indoor world with saturated hues played against pure white walls. Whether you use brilliant, intense colors or a scheme of simple summer whites, your home will welcome in the glorious light of the sun with style and verve.

summer-style
home

setting up

Begin with clean white walls to reflect as much natural light inside each room as possible. A white gallery-style background is the perfect showcase for the colors you choose to display in front of them. Or, if you like, kiss the walls with a cool tint of yellow, blue, or green—also light-reflecting backdrops. Let light flow freely through windows; cover only those that need screening for privacy. Plantation shutters or white sheers produce a tropical, warm-season look. For uncluttered drama, choose large-scale furnishings; surprisingly, a few large pieces make rooms seem bigger. Use natural materials such as wood, wicker, and stone to link your interiors to the outdoors. One kind of flooring material used throughout the house creates a feeling of continuity. You can apply the same attitude of simplicity to accessories. As with furnishings, use only a few large objects. If you go the white-and-wood route, introduce interest with large-scale textures—loose-weave curtains, heavy cotton upholstery, wicker baskets, or earthenware pottery that's roughly finished rather than slick and polished. Conceal your busy-looking electronics to promote an uncomplicated environment. Multiply space and light with large mirrors; those with dramatic frames help the pieces double as artwork. Make rooms interesting with contrasts—old and new furniture pieces, smooth and rough fabrics, soft and hard textures. Don't be afraid to mix it up!

LEFT

Double doors open the bedroom

to the garden and the sights and

sounds of nature. You can pull

together tie-on bed hangings for

privacy in the land of dreams.

OPPOSITE

Choose bold bedside art: A

Hawaiian grass skirt framed

between sheets of acrylic

plastic carries the blond color of

the wood and bamboo up the

wall and makes a warm

backdrop for an orchid or an

oversize ginger jar (left).

Another summer-style point:

Choose white shades for floor

and table lamps.

RIGHT

High-style patio furniture looks

classy enough to use inside.

With a wall of glass doors

connecting the lanai to the

house, the outdoor dining room

feels as though it's part of the

interior. Oversize glass hurricane

lamps keep the candles burning

in spite of breezes.

OPPOSITE

Thanks to the same series of

glass doors, the indoor dining

room joins the outdoors in spirit.

summer-style colors

"Pure," "clean," and "saturated" are words to describe nature's summer palette of voluptuous, fully mature hues. This is a color style for courageous, daring individuals who love intense colors and the excitement of experimenting with them. Here are three ways to dazzle your home with summer style's sizzling hues.

ONE-COLOR-PLUS-WHITE SCHEME. A pure white is the perfect foil for showcasing a favorite summer-style hue. Choose one color to brighten an accent wall or an upholstered sofa that becomes a focal point. Use large portions of white to set off the accent color.

ANALOGOUS COLOR SCHEME. Colors that fall together on paint swatch racks are relatives that form easy decorating relationships. Choose one intense hue to play a dominant role. Then add neighboring colors. Vary the intensities for a lively yet livable look.

COMPLEMENTARY COLOR SCHEME. Opposites (complements) that attract each other on the summer-style color wheel create partnerships that vibrate with intensity while maintaining a natural balance. For some color fun, try reds with greens, purples with yellows, and oranges with blues.

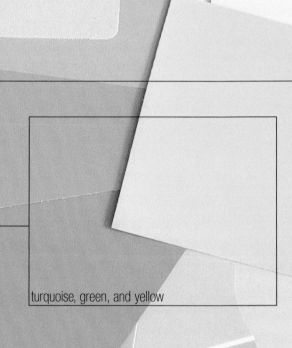

turquoise, green, and yellow

orange and white

green and fuchsia

textures and patterns

Summer's patterns and textures are twice as lively as spring's by way of bold, bright, clean shapes. Like giant sunflowers and big, show-off zinnias, summer's confident forms inspire a casual, relaxed attitude for decorating. Fun-in-the-sun cues play out in sun-drenched spots, dots, and stripes; bleached denims; carefree cottons; and bold, saturated prints.

Summer-style personalities look for blue-sky color thrills. If this is your decorating style, you'll find that a single, bold pattern in saturated hues transforms a room in seconds. Less is definitely more. The first thing to remember is to choose printed patterns that carry a base color of pure white (note the examples, *right*). Avoid fabrics and wallcoverings that have an undertone of cream, tan, or beige, shades that will kill the thrill of your pure-color trip. Use a dominating print as a room's focal point, then add the effect of texture with ministripes and dots or small overall designs. Physical texture—rough, smooth, or silky—is less defined in summer style because colors and patterns are so strong. If a room is predominantly white, however, choose a variety of textures to enliven the scheme.

Summer style and sun-washed spirits go hand in hand. You qualify for summer style if you adore reminders of your times of fun in the sun. The living room, *opposite*, began with memories of beach vacations on Cape Cod.

Snapshots that capture summer's essence can cue your color scheme. Here, the vivid contrast of a pure white egret perched against a blue sky suggests crisp white wainscoting and trim and sky blue walls. For easy-care comfort, washable denim slipcovers clothe muslin-upholstered seating. A few nautical accents underscore the theme without going overboard. In cold weather, the room beats the winter blues at their own game.

Your memory of summer vacations is a storehouse of decorating knowledge. To get started on a summer-style plan, cruise through vacation photographs from summers past. Dream up summer color and pattern schemes to enjoy at home year-round.

summer-style living

are you a summer sprite?

If so, you refuse to be tied down to anything—whether it's to a nine-to-five job or a single side of the color spectrum. You live for change, for the sparks that ignite when you put conflicting things together just to see what happens.

In the summer-style color world, opposites attract because they intensify each other. Pairing a warm color with its cool complement, such as red with green or yellow with purple, creates more energy than either color generates alone. Pure complementary schemes are easy because they're made up of only two colors. Let one color star, however, or they'll fight for dominance. For a more varied scheme, like the one in this living room, mix complementary purple and yellow with closely related partners green, blue, and orange.

In high-contrast schemes, plan places for the eye to rest. Here the white-painted coffee table and cabinet have a quieting effect. Silver metal wall panels and accessories, which the eye reads as gray, also act as neutral zones.

style points

Summer-style decorating hinges on its connection to outdoor living. If you prefer to view life from the shade of a

leafy tree or a patio table under a striped umbrella, let your home life reflect some of the same preferences. Bring

bright accents inside so you can live in the light, soak up the brilliance of the sun's rays, and delight in the

saturated hues of flowers in full bloom. No shrinking violets, please: Only the burst of a golden sunflower dripping

with seeds, a glorious red dahlia, or a shamelessly hot-pink bougainvillea will do.

1 Hang large posters that play brilliant colors against white walls. They shout out summer-style happiness. 2 Bring in fresh flowers that contrast with fabric colors in the room. Here hot pink is exciting paired with lime green. 3 Choose summer-style colors and patterns for everyday clothing; what you wear can have color thrills too. 4 With simple hooks, hang beach towels on the wall as art. 5 Create a tropical feel with furniture that has exotic leaf patterns.

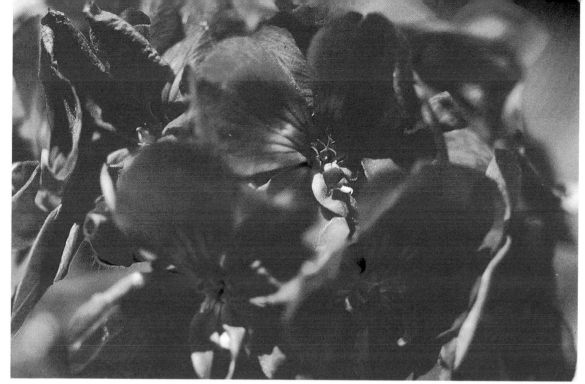

OK, so it's not your average view. But you can use this dreamy oceanside setting (and others like it) as a portfolio of decorating ideas to inspire your own outdoor dining room. Hang lanterns on a string for romantic evening light. Loosely gather a mix of wicker and natural wood chairs around a farm table. If you're starting from scratch, lay a tile or slate floor and press seashells into the grout. Use terra-cotta pots to hold brightly colored flowers, and bring lots of blue and white into play via pillow and tablecloth fabrics or dinnerware. While palm trees may be out of the question, tall green corn plants will have an equally impressive effect.

summer-style
dining

One color plus pure white equals a simple summer-style decorating plan. Blue, borrowed from the flower of the plumbago plant, inspired the scheme for this dining room. Natural bamboo folding chairs boast plumbago-colored paint, and paper lanterns with battery-operated lights hang by white strings as if lighting a poolside pavilion.

I bring fresh showers
for the thirsting flowers.
From the seas and the streams;

I bring light shade
for the leaves when laid
In their noonday dreams.

From "The Cloud" by Percy Bysshe Shelley

dining inside and out

If summer style is your look, you'll want to bring the mood of outdoor "dining rooms" indoors to enjoy year-round. While weather permits, turn porches, decks, and patios into relaxing eating places. But, when temperatures drop, it's time to bring your summer style inside to a peaceful place near a large green plant or sunny window.

To use outdoor style to brighten indoor dining, use garden furniture instead of more traditional chairs and tables. Loosely positioned, rather than placed in formal arrangements, the settings invite open seating and casual drop-by visits. Dress tables and cushions in summer-style stripes and vibrant colors. Use festive picnic ware instead of everyday glassware and china. Overall keep it simple and fresh.

style points

If you qualify as a summer-style personality, you're probably courageous with color. Or perhaps you're still timid about color and need time to practice your color-playful nature. Either way, your dining room table is a splendid platform where you can stage summer-style "color events." Here you can experiment to your heart's content, whisk away mistakes, and learn by doing. Put to work these small but bright ideas that bring style and verve to your dining room settings.

1 Replace standard white cushion covers with colorful batik fabrics. **2** Display your inspiration: Collect snippets of fabric and paint swatches that reflect your summer-style attitude and hang them with clips. **3** When mixing blue and white, use one focal-point pattern (such as the tablecloth) and add dots, stripes, and simple plaids for variety. **4** Play with color reversal: Combine a blue-on-white-background pattern with a white-on-blue one. **5** Enliven a sideboard with a show-off flower tray.

In the mind of the summer-style sleeper, going to bed is as simple as stretching out on a white beach or claiming a cloud as it drifts by. More practically, though, a hammock swinging between two trees makes a great bed. Indoors, keep the bedroom simple and airy with casual, uncomplicated furniture and accessories. Light-color bedding preserves the breezy mood regardless of the temperature outside. Whether white or solid, one-color backdrops allow bright color to have its way.

summer-style
sleeping

Lie down below a wall of flowers. To
grow this garden, buy a floral fabric
and a ready-made canvas in the
desired size at an art store. (This one
is 42 inches square.) Or, make a frame
for the fabric with individual
stretchers that fit together. In both
cases, trim the fabric with pinking
shears so the edges won't ravel.
Stretch the fabric across the canvas
or frame and wrap the edges to the
back, folding the corners gift-wrap
style. Then staple the fabric to the
back of the frame.

You can't climb into a cloud at night, but you can do the next best thing: Hop into the fantasy-laced allure of a sleeping berth. For a home with limited space, a tucked-away bed such as this provides storage and conserves space. Assembled like building blocks, a mattress and springs, boxed in with a frame of 1x8 planks, is mounted to the wall on top of side-by-side clothing chests. A narrow wall shelf caddies CDs or books, and a closet rod supports curtains that pull closed to quietly say, "Do not disturb."

create an **open-air dream**

Appropriately, the summer-style house offers lots of places for kicking back, napping, or just plain sleeping. This bamboo sofa, *opposite,* cleared of its pillow backrest and settled into a four-season porch, is a sun spot by day, a guest room by night. Wrap the seat cushion with clean white sheets, and use rice-paper panels and summer-white sheers to create privacy. Pared-down accessorizing focuses attention on a few great pieces while keeping the space from looking cluttered. White backdrops visually enlarge small spaces, allow a natural flow of sunlight, and serve as ethereal settings that provide a relaxing atmosphere. Beach mats work as area rugs here; they ground furniture arrangements and add rough texture to smooth stone-like floors.

style points

You can view nature's summer-style decorating cues everywhere, especially when you're spending your vacation

in a warm, sunny location. White-sand beaches, carnival lights, ships, flags, shells, stripes, dots, and attention-

getting patterns all translate into a decorating style that lasts all year. Adapt these summer-style ideas to make

your sleeping rooms feel as if you're always on vacation.

1 Go clean and natural; it feels good. Stack thirsty white towels on a camping stool near your bath. **2** Evoke waves and moonlight with a printed duvet cover and a paper lampshade. **3** Create a side table out of a glass urn filled with sand from the seashore and topped with a glass platter. Add more sparkle with a small chandelier hung with crystal beads. **4** End a shelf of books with a bucket of beach sand and a white starfish; if you like, throw in a specimen shell. **5** Instead of candles to light a powder room, go festive with a string of party lights orginally intended as a door drape for a college dorm room.

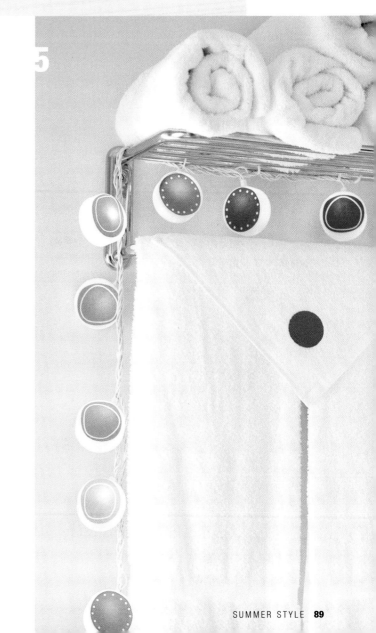

Seeing the moonlight spilling down through these trees, my heart fills to the brim with autumn.

"Seeing the Moonlight" by Ono no Komachi

Autumn's warm and bountiful style is bound to the earth by blends of mellow woods, rustic materials, and richly colored fabrics. An easy style choice to reproduce, autumn's strong, reliable, nature-inspired decorating cues support and ground a dwelling place. Here life is lived in affable surroundings that provide a place of cozy relaxation, of gathering together in good company, and of sinking into natural comforts. Turn the pages to view an abundance of autumn-style ways.

autumn style

Please accept an invitation to sink into the gracious rooms on the following pages. See whether they generate feelings of well-being and the kind of comfort that makes you want to "sit for a spell." Even if the furnishings aren't your style, notice the way colors, fabrics, and accessories work together to create an all-embracing coziness. The most striking aspects of these rooms are their cherished collections, which give the furniture, paint, and fabrics personality and soul. These items reflect the travel, humor, and spirit of people who live in harmony. If you love autumn and its gregarious style, you don't regard the act of assembling a home as an activity, or even as decorating. It's just your home. For you, creating a home is simply holding on to things you love, finding places for them, and coloring in the background to make them look their best. In autumn-style decorating, accessories come first and backgrounds last.

autumn-style
home

Draperies in autumn colors provide the foundation for

this room's toasty palette. The flowers in the fabric

suggest the terra-cotta on the walls, while the fabric's

neutral background points to a warm beige for the

natural sisal floor covering.

gathering

If you have the autumn-style gene, you know the words to the song "My Favorite Things." You gather and collect treasures the way squirrels gather nuts before the snow falls. Chances are, you own a gallery of thoughtfully framed family photographs, prefer natural-fiber fabrics, admire beautiful woods, and practice a deep respect for the earth. Your furniture and collectibles reflect your personality, and therefore make good starting points for developing comfortable decorating schemes.

arranging

Putting it all together in a pleasing manner may be tricky. That's when you should turn to autumn's style to provide a few clues. Following the lead of baskets of fruits and vegetables at the farmer's market, assemble groups of similar objects in tableaus, gathering them together to produce a better effect than they would if scattered around a room on their own. When arranging furniture, gather pieces around a central focus or hospitable spot: In living rooms, a large coffee table often draws focus; in dining rooms, it's a long, generous harvest table. Round tables are common in autumn-style kitchens; beds are the focus in autumn bedrooms. Arrangements look *away from* rather than *toward* the windows, focusing on those who gather in the room.

To create natural balance in the name of comfort, blend

casual elements with elegant ones. Relax a formal room

that features paisley and floral chintz with sisal carpet;

frame formal French doors with bamboo shades and

natural-fiber plaid curtains.

coloring in

Autumn-style curtains and upholstery contain entire palettes for creating

suitable backdrops for personal collections of furniture and accessories.

Generally autumn-style fabrics come in predominantly neutral tones with

two or three accent colors that highlight the pattern. For a no-fail color

scheme, apply the same formula to your rooms. Let the basic neutral

colors dominate floors, large seating pieces, or walls. Use the accent

colors in smaller amounts on pillows, lampshades, and special pieces in

the room. If you want to use an accent color on walls, paint only one wall

with the accent and finish the others in a neutral paint or textured

wallcovering. In addition, vary the textures on fabrics, rugs, and pillows.

A shaggy area rug and woolly needlepoint pillows, for instance, contrast

nicely with smooth chintzes and polished woods.

OPPOSITE

Believe it or not, red is a

versatile color that you can use

as a neutral. Ordinarily neutrals

are "safe" tans or beiges that

color in the largest parts of a

room such as walls or

upholstery. Here garnet

upholstery and terra-cotta walls

take on the role, warming the

dining room without

overwhelming it. These reds

infuse vitality suitable for a

convivial space.

LEFT

In the same room, a small table

holds a chess set that

perpetually invites a game.

autumn-style colors

Autumn's rich hues have a depth that exudes security and abundance. Use them in your home to build a nest of comfort, stability, and warmth. The three schemes described here will help you create color palettes from the field of choices, *right*.

ONE-COLOR-PLUS-CREAM SCHEME. Warm beiges or off-whites are present in all of autumn's brown-toned hues. For a lightweight, neutral color scheme, combine creamy white with a single favorite color such as olive green, burnt orange, or chocolate brown.

SECONDARY COLOR SCHEME. Secondary colors—violet, orange, and green—lie between primary blue, red, and yellow on the color wheel. The pairing of two secondary autumn colors results in a lively color scheme: orange with avocado, aubergine with gold, or yellow-green with violet. In autumn style, where all of the colors are so mellow, pairing greens with oranges is comfortable.

MONOCHROMATIC COLOR SCHEME. A single-color scheme is natural to autumn style, so you can base a decorating scheme on just one color—a strong gold or green, for example. Then use light and dark versions of the same color. Strong contrasts between lights and darks create energy; subtle variations subdue a mood.

yellow and cream

red-orange and avocado.

plums

textures and patterns

If you're a fan of autumn style, you're a creative sort with a sense of abundance, a love for detail, and a wealth of ideas. There's nothing stingy or flat about the way you use pattern and texture. Unlike one-dimensional decorating plans, which can be absorbed with one quick look, yours unfolds its secrets like layers of leaves over autumn's quietly regenerating flower beds. Patterns for this look often hinge on nature's leaf, fruit, or vegetable forms. So many decorative fabrics and wallcoverings are available that it's a good idea to have an overall plan in mind to help you narrow your choices and bring focus to your rooms before you delve into sample books. First, establish color schemes (see the previous pages) and carry paint samples with you when purchasing fabrics and wallcoverings. Always limit your choices to those that have beige undertones. Then choose one dominant, large-scale pattern to work with one or two smaller versions of the same motif. To balance the combination, invite a plaid into the mix. Then add one or two one-colored rustic, nubby textures that coordinate with the overall color scheme.

One way to describe autumn-style decorating is to say it's like picking apples in Eden's orchard. So many delicious orbs, so little time to enjoy them; so many beautiful objects from which to choose, so few places to display and use them. Toasty warm with the colors of ripening pumpkins and plums, autumn style is a splurge of leafy patterns, loose weaves, and inviting textures.

To live autumn style, think of your gathering room as a place that holds islands of comfort. Pull your furniture away from the wall (no more dentist's waiting room) and arrange the pieces in small groups on area rugs to define them. In close groups such as this, connections are inspired, and your guests won't have to shout across the room to be heard. When placing furniture, allow at least 18 inches of space for walking between armchairs and coffee tables. Also make sure your comfort islands don't impede the traffic through the room. It's better to have traffic flow around a conversation group than through it.

autumn-style living

Burnished greens, golds, reds, and browns epitomize the autumn style. When included in a sunny butter-yellow and white setting, the result is a hybrid spring/fall style. What makes this work? Commonalities both styles share: similar warm color choices and the tendency to gather an abundance of desirable objects.

No spring, nor summer
beauty hath such grace,
As I have seen in one
autumnal face.

"The Autumnal" from *Elegies* by John Donne

To assemble a luxurious reading alcove of the autumn-style sort, first explore leafy prints. If you have a bump-out or dormer, hang floor-to-ceiling curtain panels on swing-arm drapery rods to create a sense of snug enclosure. Although the "rules" dictate the use of only one large-scale print per room, two large prints coexist peacefully here, blended by a common color palette. Simpler one- and two-color coordinating prints layer the curtains and hang as a poufy balloon shade. Plain polished-cotton pillows give the eye a rest from all the pattern and further link the two large prints.

In a room that lacks a fireplace or any inherent architectural character, you can invent a focal point with a boldly colored accent wall and bookcase units that hold a treasury of titles. This pairing—a strong, rustic wall color and an imposing piece of furniture in front of it—draws attention away from the room's boxy shape and helps alter perception of the space. If you like, you can pull some of the accent color into the room by using accessories. But if you want to direct eyes to the focal point, accessorize in neutral beige, ivory, and black.

1

2

style points

Go ahead, be sentimental. It's all part of autumn's gather-together style. Celebrate your good fortune of family and

friends by including them in your decorating scheme. They'll love seeing photos and other representations of

themselves (the fish Dad whittled, the clay bowl your sister made) in the rooms of your home. Scan these pages

for small ways to create the detailed look of a home graced by those who come and go through your front and back

doors, by freedom to express yourself within your own walls, and by many days lived in comfort and ease.

1 "Build" a clever and convenient chair-side table by placing a small treasure chest on a four-legged tray. **2** Scour antiques shops to find letters from old signs or printing presses; then monogram a mantel tableau with family initials. **3** Keep comfort underfoot with leaf-patterned rugs; they'll remind you of dry, rustling leaves.

4 Welcome family home with familiar photographs; include a mirror so they can check their reflections. **5** Warm a table with bittersweet and hang cards on the branches with bright ribbons.

The exuberant nature of autumn's style inspires over-the-top decorating. While simplicity and sparsity represent the nature of summer and winter schemes, the season of harvest vibrates with rich abundance. To go with autumn's flow, indulge in exciting pattern mixes, warm color schemes, and layers of fabric. Large-scale florals, country checks, and vintage tablecloths evoke autumn in a cottage-style breakfast spot, *opposite*. Instead of adhering to a strictly red-and-green complementary scheme, accents hop around the color wheel: yellow-green, yellow, and yellow-orange touches taken from both the draperies and the tablecloth make for harmonious details.

autumn-style dining

when you're torn between two styles

You're right, this autumn-style dining room doesn't exactly fit the profile. It has a generous harvest table and cozy chairs, but the room seems a bit cool and sparse for the abundant, gregarious ways of autumn. Why? This room is a hybrid of two styles—autumn and summer—and proves that you can blend two styles you love and come up with decorating solutions as original as your fingerprints. To blend styles, a neutral backdrop is the easiest way to begin (you can change wall color later if you like). Then split the differences between the seasons and let a little of each style have a say in the room. For example, make the autumn-style dining table the focus, but between meals, arrange the chairs away from the table to make the room more summer simple. Enjoy your accessories (autumn), but keep them to a minimum (summer).

A handsome, classic-style light fixture floats like a harvest moon over the table. Elaborate wall sconces promise warm candlelit evenings when the weather turns gray or days grow short. Uncovered, the windows nod to the open-to-the-sky summer side of the room's two-season style. Richly textured table and chair coverings add a layer of autumnal warmth.

indulging your senses

If autumn's style appeals to you, you're a nurturer. It's probably safe to say that you love organic vegetables, golden retrievers, wood fires, and hand-knitted sweaters. More than likely, your favorite smell is bread baking in an oven, and you adore throwing parties in your kitchen. Like Mom's apple pie, autumn's warm neutrals, peach tones, and buttery yellows are the comfort foods of the color spectrum. They blend easily into the background, yet beckon you to touch. At the same time, they rouse appetites so they're appropriate colors for dining rooms. Another aspect: Use them to suggest a safe, snug feeling in a room with small windows, northern exposures, or woodsy views. To assure visual interest, layer on textures such as smooth wood furniture, rustic baskets, and woven linens.

style points

Like the season that inspires it, autumn-style dining is both robust and fragile, fleeting yet enduring. Once a meal

has come and gone, only the memory of it remains. When you set your table, remember this: Once nature's rich

harvest of colors has faded to brown, interesting textures remain. Be conscious of color at your table and

concentrate on a menu of textures that makes your meals worth remembering. Here are a few tabletop ideas that

suggest ways to bring interesting and enduring textures to your table.

1 Dry fallen leaves in a phone book and save them in brown paper bags to slip under glass dinner plates any time of the year. **2** Tie sheer ribbon bows on stemware to celebrate a special occasion. **3** Use a polished tree round as a server for a hearty, rustic loaf of bread. **4** Cut crisp, fragile hydrangea blooms to use in waterless vases all year-round. **5** Mimic the beauty of fallen leaves with small leafy branches at place settings.

Creating an autumn-style sleeping nest is a bit like weaving a web. With delicate threads of imagination, you spin a few of your favorite things into a beautiful design while you dream of settling in among your prizes. In the intimate room within a room, *opposite,* the bed's metal headboard is slipcovered in the same sheer fabric used for the bed hangings. Dessert plates decorated with twenty different varieties of hand-painted flowers fill the wall with pattern. Another collection—one-of-a-kind pillows—crowds the bed and promises comfort for a tired body. Like most web-weaving collectors, you may find the thrill of the hunt as appealing as any special catch. For you, a collection is never complete; another favorite object waits to be discovered at the next turn in the road.

autumn-style
sleeping

If you like, you can take "style by nature" quite literally as this bedroom does. Made from the branches of trees chopped down in the woods, the bed is the focal point that provides the rustic character in this suburban bedroom. Twig tables, benches, and a plant stand expand the theme. Such rugged textures might suggest cowboy motifs for fabrics, but if they aren't a natural choice for you, opt for large-scale florals, stripes, and plaids to accompany the weighty furnishings. Green plants bring to mind the leafy parts of twigs and tree trunks, and they balance the rugged textures and stiff lines of the furniture.

style points

Nothing matches a bedside table or the walls near your bed for opportunities to enjoy your most precious

possessions at close range. Here, in the most private part of the house, feel free to celebrate the intimate side of

yourself by keeping the items that mean the most to you where they can prompt your thoughts and set you to

dreaming. Let these five ways to practice autumn style inspire your bedside manners.

1 Start with a bedside lamp and its warm pool of light, then surround it with natural treasures. **2** For a comfortingly quiet piece of art, frame a small square of handmade papyrus or paper in a shadow box. **3** Illuminate a mail-order leaf-printed wall sconce to symbolize your seasonal decorating style. **4** To keep decorating plans forever near, arrange fabric pieces and sample swatches under glass on your desktop. **5** Lean up against a hand-dyed pillow covered in burnished browns.

My mother once said to me, "When one sees the tree in leaf one thinks the beauty is in its leaves, and then one sees the bare tree."

"The Bare Tree" by Samuel Menashe

When you want home to be a place of quiet meditation and retreat from a hectic world, winter style may be the best decorating prescription for you. Here all is calm, all is serene—at least on the surface. At the core of the style, a fire burns brightly and high-contrast materials keep it alive. Like nature's season of dormancy, winter style's neutral hues, patterns, and textures heal and content while they revitalize your spirits. Turn the pages for ways to assemble this soothing look.

winter style

When autumn rolls up its giddy carpet of colors and fades away, winter blows in to blanket the earth and lull it to sleep. Or, not quite. Beneath the soft, snowy covering, life merely shifts from survive to revive. While spring's flowery decorating cues are easy to spot, winter's interior inspirations are more subtle; they come into view with smooth ice underfoot, dark tree trunks in distant fields, delicate frost on windows, and wet snowflakes on your nose. To welcome winter style into your home, think of your interior as a safe haven from the storm, where furnishings face inward and gather round the fire. If you have no fireplace, you can interpret the symbolic heart(h) of your home in other inviting ways, which you will encounter in this chapter. Turn the pages to learn how you can conjure winter's soul to life inside your house, no matter what your home's style of architecture or its furnishings. These ideas work all year.

winter-style
home

Winter's natural decorating materials are honest and true, exposed to the elements. Glaze your rooms with glass, an ice look-alike that expresses winter's honesty. Mirrors, tabletops, and windows are the most obvious ways; don't forget glass lamp bases and desktops too.

setting up

Winter's safe haven is easy to create if you begin with a neutral interior. Select your favorite grayed-down color and spread variations of it from room to room and wall to wall. Winter-style floor coverings are smooth icelike slate, ceramic tile, or polished hardwood—cool in summer and warmed by area rugs in cold weather. Marble or stone fireplace surrounds fit in perfectly. Snow-white or charcoal kitchen countertops create crisp, quiet lines. As in winter's stark world, let the structure of your furnishings show, reveal the "bones," see the steel, hide nothing. Use strong vertical and horizontal lines (walls, windows, floors, and some furniture). Then, because winter style is also one of contrasts, counter the rigid scheme with a few curves. Round mirrors and tables offer the greatest effect. To further soften a room's hard edges, choose curved furniture shapes upholstered in soft fabrics. Love your bare windows: Treat them with blinds or roller shades for privacy's sake, or use draperies to "frame" views within expanses of cold glass. Avoid complex fabric patterns, lavish draperies, and fussy, feminine folds.

You can give the artwork on your walls the glow of a

hearth by directing recessed lights onto them. Relate art

to furniture below with everyday, utilitarian objects such

as the pitchers and bowls on the buffet.

accessorizing

Beloved accessories and precious artwork are the life and spirit of a winter-style room.

If you're a true winter's soul, you warm to simple, elegant pieces that tell a tale and

humanize a room. You admire all handcrafted objects, whether they're turned on a

potter's wheel or blown out of a glob of glass in a glassblower's studio. You collect

subtle, frosted-glass urns and tableware, ceramic vases, and unusual ethnic art. Unlike

adherents of other nature styles, you don't collect in great quantities—just enough to

zap a sleeping room with a bit of fiery color or a spirited memento you picked up on

your travels. Occasionally you find a piece of art furniture to serve at bedside or beside

a reading chair. Your middle name is "editor," for you know when to stop if you've

come close to stepping over the line of elegant simplicity and subtle sophistication.

The ideal winter-style bedroom has a fireplace, but unless you live in a very old house (or a very new one), yours probably doesn't. To turn up the heat for a restful night, you can substitute a hot shot of blaze-colored upholstery, then give your legs a lift with an ottoman that also works as a table or tray.

LEFT

A handsome four-poster bed provides shelter for body and soul. Line your bed with a luxurious fabric "ceiling" for better soundproofing and a cozier feeling.

winter-style colors

Sophisticated, subtle spirits find pleasure in winter's cool palette. Drained of intensity and grayed down to the minimum, the field of choices, *right*, offers a somewhat neutral range that comes to life with a single, calculated swish of cranberry or icy blue-green.

evergreen and cranberry

COMPLEMENTARY COLOR SCHEME. Winter's natural opposites, the evergreens and berry reds, combine as accent hues in otherwise neutral rooms. Consider other winter-style pairings such as teal blue and rust, ivory and amethyst as well.

WHITE-ON-WHITE COLOR SCHEME. The most elegant of color schemes is inspired by winter's snow-white storms, rabbit furs, and frosty window panes. Made up of variations on white, the plan is simple: white plus any variation of white such as cream, snow, sheepskin, seashell, or bone. To make sure this scheme doesn't put you to sleep, toss in an accent-red and vary the textures.

MONOCHROMATIC COLOR SCHEME. The contrasting darks and lights of winter's palette are easy to combine. All you need is one color and several dark and light variations of it. For example, combine a mid-tone blue-gray, a lighter blue-gray, and a dark one.

white on white

steel grays

textures and patterns

Low-key, faded patterns and mysterious, undercover textures are major players in a serene and cerebral winter-style color scheme. With their whisper-soft sheers, barely there embossings, and ice-smooth tiles, they have the power to cool down color chaos and calm tattered nerves. A touch of green velvet or snowy damask brings to mind the scent of evergreen, the silhouettes of leafless oaks, and the swoosh of ice skates crossing a mirrored pond.

When choosing patterns and textures for winter style, be sure to choose a wide variety. Except for accents, winter-style colors are muted enough to put you to sleep, so they need the company of interesting patterns and textures that play soft music in silent spaces. Avoid large-patterned fabrics and wallcoverings with loud, contrasting colors; they belong to summer's exuberant style. For winter style's healing quality, combine a silk brocade with suede or cashmere wool. Try a woven jacquard with a fuzzy chenille, or a pale leaf-print chintz with a satin-and-matte damask. When it comes to upholstery fabrics, avoid those that are hard to clean or costly to care for.

Lady Stairs
Two   Close

Nothing says winter style better than a hearth and its comforting fire, a classic icon. The hearth's presence in a room sends an immediate message of warmth and renewal. It's also a natural when it comes to focal points, second in popularity only to the looming modern-day big-screen television set. Today family rooms that don't have fireplaces substitute televisions, which offer their own form of warmth and fascinating light.

You can create comfortable winter-style living quarters with a minimum of furnishings: two easy chairs and a coffee table suffice. Create a relaxed air by covering the chairs in winter-white wide-wale corduroy, washable denim, or softened canvas. Then add elements of surprise to please the heart or tease the mind. The result adds up to a room like the one shown. Turn the pages for different interpretations of winter-style living.

winter-style
living

For centuries, leaves, trees, birds, and animals have inspired artists to design decorative patterns for use at home. For winter style, choose a pairing of "fire" colors—the red and gold used here—in patterned materials to fill a traditional setting of intimate proportions.

winter plus autumn

In the world of natural decorating, you can have your cake and eat it too. Those who have a winter-style home dressed in sophisticated neutral colors but secretly long for a tiny, intimate, autumn-style space for a "fireside" sitting room needn't despair. Subtle prints in a warm-as-flame color scheme evoke both autumn's toasty tones and the fire built into the heart of winter. Begin with a patterned rug or a dominant fabric or wallcovering. Then choose supporting prints and solids in the same colors. With a patterned background, use uncomplicated, medium-dark pieces of furniture that won't jar the setting. Select the colors and patterns in close range to each other to maintain a serene comfort level. (High-contrasting black-and-white toile, on the other hand, would produce visual chaos for the winter-style mind.)

Dark and light contrasts, stunning as bare trees in a snow-covered field, rapidly put their stamp on a room. This living area's vintage bus-destination signs easily capture focal-point status and beg you to ask questions about them. When you assemble a serene winter-style living room from grayed-down neutral colors and refined textures, it's a good idea to take the edge off the room's reserve with a sublimely captivating brainteaser or two that keep the room from feeling colorless.

Come, lovely Morning
rich in frost
On iron, wood and glass
From "The Silver Hours" by W.H. Davies

style points

Like summer's style, winter-style living is easy. But, aside from the simplicity and frequent use of white, that's

probably all they have in common. While summer-style living is carefree, winter-style's studied serenity has a plan

for rest and renewal. Winter-style living is about resting the body and renewing the mind with small decorative

touches that entertain and bring meaning to a room. To live a little more easily, use these winter-style touches

that engage the minds and please the eyes of those who share your spaces.

1 Highlight the subtle tones in winter art with a guided picture light. 2 Play up natural contrasts; place rough earthy elements inside smooth bowls. 3 Heighten color contrasts; upholster a dark bench with a light fabric. 4 Fire up an all-white room with red accents that represent winter style's rosy, regenerating world beneath the snow. 5 Combine fire and ice: Plant candles in a container filled with faux ice cubes that won't melt.

Winter's quiet ways imbue dining rooms with a mood that's serene—but not sleepy. Just because winter-style rooms are cloaked in grayed-down neutrals or sophisticated winter whites doesn't mean they've gone into hibernation. Casual or studied, loosely assembled or tightly ordered, they carry a torch for wit, a touch of humor, or a bright bit of color that begs a smile. In this dining room, a fuchsia ruffle adorns traditional draperies to make them less serious, the bird's-nest chandelier adds a touch of humor, and vintage French tea towels are casually dropped over the tops of dining chairs as impromptu slipcovers. Urns of bare branches celebrate winter's leafless nature.

winter-style dining

Whether it's summer or winter, California or Maine, a long corridor or open lanai can carry the earmarks of winter-style decorating. Winter style exists in light and dark contrasts, neutral backdrops, the subtle punch of warm color, and intimate settings. To divide a long, spiritless, tunnel-shape space into small, protected sections, hang burlap from iron rods attached to the ceiling. To give the panels an elegant winter-style air, trim them with linen borders. If there's no hearth to lend a cozy atmosphere, burn candles in a chandelier.

When dinner is presented in front of a crackling fire, it's impossible not to feel cozy and content. Position a coffee table a safe distance from the hearth, and surround it with floor pillows. Not everyone is comfortable sitting on the floor so pull up a few easy chairs as well. Keep the ambient lighting low to let the firelight shine, but illuminate a nearby table lamp to help guests find their seats. A tray-style table with raised sides helps corral mealtime necessities. Be thoughtful when adding items with height: You don't want to block anyone's view of the blaze.

style points

When you're a winter-style personality, engaging conversation isn't all you bring to the dinner table. Always at work, your decorating wit seeks ways to entertain the eye with light and dark contrasts, playing rustic elements against refined ones, or turning natural, everyday materials into pleasant surprises for those who come to dine. Whether dinner is casual or formal, off-the-cuff or planned in advance, setting your table is an event you enjoy for the pleasure it brings. Try a few of these small but effective winter-style touches.

1 Assemble a centerpiece in a wide salad bowl with candles, black beans, and white beans. 2 It's a black-tie affair: The napkin keeps a sweating water pitcher dry. 3 Arrange a buffet with frosted glass and white linens for a winter-style look year-round. 4 To dress up fireside take-out, use a steamer filled with smooth stones as a centerpiece; serve chopsticks in white rice. 5 For winter-white elegance, set a table with gleaming china and refined white linens.

Akin to hibernating bears, winter-style sleepers love a special world of voluminous depths that promises recuperation and regeneration. Weather permitting, billowy beds of goose down and fresh, white cotton sheets are the ideal; however, when the air temperatures rise, white linens with padded textures or muted colors and patterns perform the same winter-style magic. This delicately turned iron bed frame dresses in winter's grayed-down hues, a lightweight version of winter's usual depths of goose down comforters, blankets, and pillows.

winter-style sleeping

Plumped with goose down or filled with foam, pillows are an essential ingredient in feathering the nest. Pile them up to express the look and feel of winter style and to give yourself comfy support for sitting up or snuggling in. Dressed all in white, a mix of decorative styles harmonizes. In this grouping, clean-edged modern, ruffled country, and big European-size classic pillows ease body and soul. For more winter-style pillow ideas, turn to pages 160 and 161.

LEFT

Snow-white is the color of escapes into serenity, as if white linens fold the cares of a wearied world into a comforting drift. For symbolic shelter, curtain a poster bed with frosty (sheer) tie-on panels originally intended for windows. When mixing white pillows, compare fabrics closely to ensure consistent color. Standard-size pillowcases, the easiest option, keep cleaning and care at a minimum. Smooth pillow covers provide little textural interest, though, so blend decorative details such as quilted surfaces, crisp welting, and soft ruffles into the scheme.

enhancing white spaces

In Scandinavian lands, where the winter sun seldom shines, white is revered for its ability to reflect and enhance the scant available light. But when white visually freezes a room, warm it with special effects. In this bedroom, a crimson spread and pillow shams invigorate a basic background of white walls and fabrics like a branch of holly berries on a drift of snow. To further banish the chill, large door mirrors encourage glitter and glamour and reflect natural light. Keep window coverings as simple as possible to let in the sun. Include soft curves, such as the scalloped edges of this bed's matelassé covering and the swag of the shade, which add grace and elegance to the rectangular room.

style points

If winter-style decorating appeals to your senses, you probably love frosted windows, steamy saunas, and spirit-

lifting accents, especially in the rooms where you sleep. Indulge in drifts of white, whether they come in the form

of quilted comforters, rice-paper shades, filmy cotton curtains, feather "potpourris," or delicate porcelain bowls.

Here are five ways to spice up your sleeping quarters with the fresh, clean power of ski-slope white.

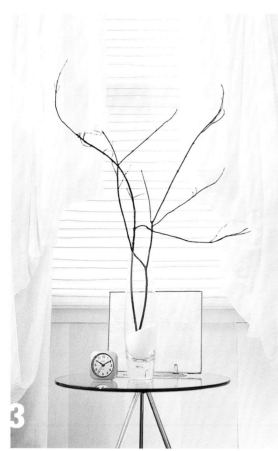

1 White isn't just white; it comes in a variety of tones and textures. If you vary them enough, you can use them together. 2 Play the energy of dark chocolate walls off crisp white furnishings and trim in a bedroom office. 3 Capture the beauty of winter trees settled into snow: Plant bare twigs in salt. 4 Pair menswear pinstripe fabrics with snowflake dots for a sophisticated mix of pillows. 5 Warm a guest room with a white porcelain washing bowl.

project primer

Here you'll find 24 window treatments to express your natural style.

autumn

winter

spring style shimmery & sheer

If you're a spring-style spirit who's in love with sunlight, you're attracted to open, airy spaces with lots of windows that invite natural light into your rooms.

In a room with many windows, light control is desirable, especially during the summer months or in southern locales. For the best light control, cover your windows with blinds equipped with wands that turn the blades of the shades to a comfortable level.

For beauty's sake, add sheer ready-made panels over the shades and tie them back in graceful swags. If you're an elegant spring-style type, choose sheers with shiny-and-matte designs like the striped panels shown, *right*. If you're the casual type, plain cream-white sheer panels might work better. Keep the tiebacks in place with cleats or decorative holders attached to the wall. You can find a variety of window-hanging hardware in fabric stores, home furnishings stores, and home centers.

Place seating near windows covered

with sheers where you can enjoy

relaxing hours spent in filtered

sunlight. The best light for applying

makeup is natural light, so it's a good

idea to place a dressing table

near a window.

Yellow ready-made tab-top panels embellished with a pattern of white silk-screened apple blossom branches cast an ethereal atmosphere. To make them, you'll need a 9×12-inch silk-screen printing kit, available at arts and crafts supply stores.

silk-screen print spring style

To prepare the screen for printing, detach it from its base. Enlarge the branch design, *above,* on a copy machine until the branch fills an 8½×11-inch sheet of paper. Lay the screen over the image top side up, and trace the design onto the screen with a soft lead pencil. With a small art brush, fill in the shapes inside the lines with the kit's drawing fluid. While you do this, make sure the screen is elevated; it must not touch the table. Allow it to dry in a level position.

Mix the kit's screen filler. Spoon it onto the screen on the same side as the drawing fluid. Use the kit's squeegee to spread the filler evenly over the screen. One pass should be enough—too much could compromise the image. Dry the screen in a level position. Then spray *cold* water on both sides of the screen and gently brush away the drawing fluid with a toothbrush. Dry in a level position with the bottom side up.

Before you print on the curtain, wash, dry, and iron it. Lay it on a flat surface over a piece of waxed paper where you plan to print the image. Lay the screen flush side down over the surface. Put a spoonful of white textile ink on the screen. Holding the screen in place, squeegee ink up and down the screen until the image is filled. Carefully lift the screen, holding the fabric in place. Repeat in rows across the curtain panel. Dry in a hanging position. When dry, set the prints with a hot iron on the cotton setting; place a cloth between the iron and fabric to prevent damage. Wash the screen immediately after use.

spring style hard and soft

Glass drawer knobs (either antique or reproduction) take the place of Shaker pegs for hanging the valance. Use hanger bolts (doubled-ended screws) to attach the knobs to the window frame, spacing them about 6 inches apart.

A hefty plate rail and a frilly dotted-swiss valance give this shuttered window its yin-and-yang appeal. For the plate rail, cut a 1×4 board slightly wider than the window frame (allow for a 2-inch overhang at each end). Rout a plate ridge on top of it before attaching it to the window frame with screws. Using a miter box to cut the corners, add dentil molding to hide the joint. Paint the plate rail and molding to match the window frame.

For the valance cut scallop-edge dotted swiss the desired depth by the width of the window, plus 1 inch for each knob and 2 inches for hems. Narrowly hem the upper and side edges. Using a pin, mark the position for each knob. Measure an extra inch of valance between each knob to create a draped effect. Turn under the raw end of a strand of cording and topstitch it to the upper edge of the valance using a zigzag stitch. As you reach each point where a knob is positioned, loop the cord to form a hanger. Turn under the remaining raw end. Hang the valance loops from the knobs.

faintly formal spring style

Sewing formal pleated draperies is an advanced skill; pleating tapes get the job done a little more easily. Manufacturers of the tapes indicate how much tape to buy based on the style of the pleater tape you choose. You'll need to purchase one additional pleat section for each curtain panel you make. For each panel, purchase 54-inch-wide fabric. To determine the length needed, measure the window from the top of the rod to the floor and add 10 inches.

To make an unlined panel, hem the sides: Fold under the raw edges ¼ inch, press, fold under again 2 inches, and press. Stitch along the first folded edge. Turn the top raw edge over 3 inches. Follow the manufacturer's instructions to fasten the tape to the top of the curtain. To hem the panel, hang it on the curtain rod, turn under the bottom edge of the curtain so it just meets the floor, and pin. Remove the panel from the rod; press the fold. Measure 6 inches from the fold and trim the excess. Turn the raw edge of the curtain to meet the folded edge. Press. Refold the hem, making angle folds at the corners. Hemstitch the folded edges.

What's that fun and funky decorative flourish on top of this window frame? The faux mirror is actually painted directly on the wall with acrylic paint. It lengthens the window and gives it a more graceful shape. You can also fasten a painted plywood cutout to the wall or, for true authenticity, attach a small dresser mirror that you purchased at a flea market.

spring style **ribbon dance**

When purchasing as much ribbon as this door drape requires, explore crafts supply stores for bulk supplies of florist's ribbon. It's less expensive than the silk ribbons you'll find in fabric stores.

Light as a balloon on a string, this romantic ribbon curtain is perfect for an open doorway, where the breeze can blow through it.

To make it, buy an adjustable tension rod that fits the width of the doorway. You'll also need enough 2-inch-wide florist's ribbon to measure 10 times the height of the doorway plus an extra 2 feet for tying loose knots.

With scissors, cut the total length of the ribbon into five equal strips. Hang the tension rod in the door opening and loop the ribbon strips over the rod. Holding the two sides of each strip together, loosely tie them in a simple knot. Arrange the ribbon bands on one side of the opening. To trim the ends, fold each end of the ribbon strip in half lengthwise and make a diagonal cut from the folded edge to the selvage edges.

sunny side up *spring style*

To create a neat transition between the sheer and opaque fabrics, turn under raw edges in a narrow French seam (see photograph *below*). Choosing a colored, patterned sheer provides a bit more privacy on top than a plain, light-colored sheer does.

Let the sun shine in while retaining your privacy. With a translucent top third to let in the light and opaque bottom two-thirds for privacy, these panels combine sheer and lightweight fabrics. To make a panel, join fabric lengths with a narrow French seam: With wrong sides facing, sew a ⅜-inch seam. Trim the seam allowance to less than ¼ inch. Fold the fabric with right sides facing, placing the seam at the edge. Stitch about ⅝ inch from the first seam, encasing the raw edges. Hem the remaining edges with narrow hems. Then attach skinny ties to the top of the panel and tie them to the curtain rods.

summer style **nautical and nice**

To find nautical cleats, check the Yellow Pages for local boat-supply stores. They usually carry a variety of sizes, or they can order them for you. While you're there, buy the nautical cord for the curtain rod.

No-sew projects appeal to summer-style types, and here's one everyone will love. It's made with a shower curtain that has grommets that make it easy to hang on a curtain rod. Hang it on a regular rod for straighter lines or hang it on a cord to give it a breezier nonchalance.

With large screws (or toggle bolts if you can't screw into studs), fasten the cleats to the wall 6 inches above the window frame and 4 inches from each side. Thread the cord through the grommets and wrap the ends of the cord around the cleat, nautical style. If the tension isn't enough the first time, release and rewrap the cord until you get the look you want.

Trim the ends of the cord and tie them off in a simple knot.

Everything about summer says "Easy does it" and "Anything goes." If you love the colors and patterns on a summer-weight bedcover, why not use it as a window cover too?

All you need to do is sew a rod pocket on the back of the spread at one end. To make a rod pocket, measure the width of the spread and purchase enough wide hem-facing tape to cover it. Pin the hem facing (raw edges inside) to the back of the spread 2 inches from the edge. Sew along both of the folds of the tape to make a channel through which you can insert a curtain rod.

Put the curtain on the rod (use a length of garden bamboo for a summer touch) and fasten it into the wall brackets.

Antiques fairs and flea markets often offer racks of fabric furnishings for very little money. Search through the piles and you just might come up with a good candidate for this curtain idea. Lightweight pieces with interesting finished edges, such as this summer seersucker bedspread with a scallop edge, work best.

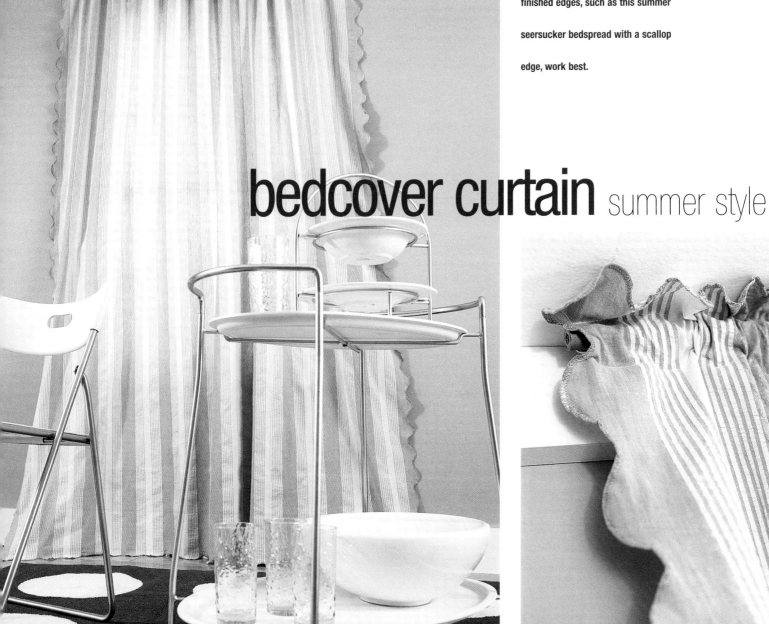

bedcover curtain summer style

summer style **sailworthy**

After the shade is in place, thread rope loosely

through the grommets. Knot the cord on each end

and slide a metal curtain rod through the loops to

weight the shade. Make sure the rod rests just

above the sill when the shade is lowered and its

ends align with the edge of the window so it

doesn't bang against the glass.

With the addition of grommets and rope, this seersucker shade gets a sailworthy look. A metal curtain rod lashed to the bottom weights it down so it hangs properly.

Cut a seersucker fabric panel to fit exactly inside the window, adding 3 inches to the width and 1½ inches to the length. Press under the side and bottom edges ¼ inch, then turn under a 1½-inch hem. Topstitch. Repeat for the top, making a 1½-inch rod pocket. Sew ring tape found at fabric stores to the back of the shade along the outer edges. Space grommets 4 inches apart along the lower edge. Cut a 1×1 board to fit inside the rod pocket and slide it in place. Insert screw eyes through the fabric and board at about 8-inch intervals. Tie a shade cord to the bottom ring on each side. On one side, run the cord through the rings and all screw eyes. On the other side, run it through the rings and outer screw eye only. Mount the shade with small L-brackets. Secure the cords to a curtain cleat fastened on one side of the window frame.

Measure and cut oxford-cloth fabric panels so together they total one and a half times the width of the window, then add 3 inches to the width of each panel. For length, measure and cut so the panels are the desired finished length plus 6 inches for the hem and a casing for the curtain rod. Hemstitch the long outer edges of the panels. Press back 2 inches of each inner edge, right sides facing. Press under ½ inch on the raw edge and topstitch along both fold lines to form a false placket. To make the rod casing at the top, fold over the raw edges ½ inch and press. Fold over again 3½ inches; press. Machine-stitch along the first folded edge and 1 inch in from the second fold. At the bottom, hem panels narrowly. Using a buttonhole attachment, make buttonholes in the placket of one panel, spacing them 6 to 8 inches apart. Sew corresponding buttons to the other panel. Make 3-inch-wide tiebacks from 7-inch-wide strips of matching fabric.

Button up a bit of dress-down style with these oxford-cloth curtains, which feature a false placket and real shirt buttons and buttonholes. This faux placket technique works only on true oxford cloth that has no right or wrong sides.

buttoned down summer style

summer style **have a ball**

Beaded-ball fringe mimics the pattern of sheer dotted swiss. Your trim should match the curtain panel both in visual and actual weight. A too-heavy trim, such as a thick fringe, may drag down lightweight fabric and distort the graceful drape of the curtain.

Cut a panel of dotted-swiss fabric that's two to three times the width of your window and 6 inches longer. Narrowly hem both long edges, top, and bottom. Fold and press the top 3½ inches of the panel, wrong sides facing, to allow for a 2-inch-wide rod pocket with a 1½-inch header above it. Sew along the hemmed edge and 2 inches above it. Topstitch ball fringe to one side of the panel. Slide the curtain rod through the pocket and hang the curtain.

To create the tieback, use a piece of string to determine the height and angle of the drawstring (this one aligns with windowpanes when the curtain is drawn). Mark the angle with a water-soluble fabric marker on the curtain. Remove the string and curtain. Sew individual rings or ring tape (found at fabric stores) along this angle on the back of the curtain (remove marks with water). Run a shade cord through the rings and tie it to the ring near the trimmed edge.

Hang the curtain and attach a cup hook or small cleat to the window frame as an anchor for the cord.

If you'd rather not work too hard at stitching up full-size curtains and privacy isn't an issue, casually decorate a kitchen window with brightly colored squares of fabric the size of dinner napkins. Or purchase ready-made napkins in graphic summer-style patterns.

To make these curtains, cut 18-inch squares of fabric. With matching thread, make narrow rolled hems around all sides of each square. To make a rolled hem, fold the raw edge over ¼ inch and press it with a steam iron. Then fold over the edges another ¼ inch and machine-stitch close to the first fold. Press.

To hang the squares, fit adjustable tension rods inside the window frame. Then fold the squares over the rods and pull the corners from side to side until you have a pleasing tossed-on look. Note: The curtains shown here fit 36-inch-wide windows. For larger windows, increase the size of the squares.

hanky panky summer style

Add to the fun of this window treatment by covering your kitchen table with coordinating fabrics hemmed in a similar fashion to the curtains. You also can fray edges of fabric squares such as the one lining the fruit basket here. Colorful plates propped up on display stands add zest and pattern to the space.

autumn style **old is new again**

Vintage curtain panels from an antiques shop spruce up a modern-day window. Use them as you find them or alter the length as needed. Hang them as bands of autumn color and pattern to frame an otherwise plain window treatment.

Search antiques shops for inexpensive fabrics from bygone eras.

If you need to alter the length of two curtain panels, leave the hems as they are and trim the tops one inch longer than the desired length. Hem the top of each panel by folding over ¼ inch twice and machine-stitching close to the edge with matching thread.

To hang the panels, purchase two packages of metal clips from the curtain hardware section of a home center store. Then buy a bamboo stick for a curtain rod (you can find bamboo at import stores and garden shops). Slip the rings onto the rod and clip the curtain panels to the rings. Hang the rod on curtain brackets or balance it on open shutters at each side of the window.

Damask makes a decorative impact in unexpected places. One idea is to apply it to the wall below the chair rail, as a wainscot stand-in; the other is to use it as a trim for ready-made curtains.

To embellish standard ready-made curtain panels like these, cut 12-inch-wide damask strips for side borders and 5-inch-wide strips for edging the tops of the panels. To determine the lengths for each, measure the actual widths and lengths of the ready-made panels; then add 12 inches for folding. Fold strips in half lengthwise, press, and open out. Fold under all raw edges 1 inch; press. For each panel, open the side border; on the front of the outer side of the panel, match the raw edge to the finished edge of the curtain panel; pin and sew together along the fold. Fold the remaining part of the border strip to the back side of the panel, matching it to the front. Hand-sew it to the back of the panel. Repeat this process to edge the curtain top and the outer side of additional panels. Sew rings to the panels for hanging.

A damask wainscot creates a richer look than paint or wallpaper. To secure fabric to the wall, roll or brush on clear, nonstaining vinyl adhesive or cellulose paste. Then press fabric in place, smoothing wrinkles as you go. Cover raw edges with wood moldings.

damask to the border autumn style

autumn style mini panels

This window is decorated with three fabric panels on each side of a set of sheers. For spring and summer, only the rose panels border the sheers for a lighter look. In fall and winter, the narrow striped panels are arranged on each side of a rose-printed panel.

With a wardrobe of narrow fabric side panels that coordinate with the other fabrics in your room, you can change the look of your window from season to season.

To make a panel, measure and cut 24-inch-wide lengths of fabric. Cut them 8 inches longer than the desired finished length to allow for a hem and a rod casing. To roll-hem the long edges of the panels, fold the raw edges under ¼ inch and press. Fold again to hide the raw edges; press. Topstitch along the inner fold.

To make the rod casing at the top, fold over the raw edges ½ inch and press. Fold again 3½ inches; press. Machine-stitch along the inner fold and 1 inch in from the outer fold (to make the ruffle at the tops of the panels).

To hem the bottoms, fold raw edges under ½ inch and press. Fold again 3½ inches and press. Machine-stitch along the inner (first) folded edge.

To unify two different curtain panels, use a repeating element. Small grommets applied randomly to the gauze panels mimic the large grommets on the corduroy ones. Purchase a grommet kit—the kind you can install with only a hammer and a block of wood—from the notions section of a fabric store.

go with grommets autumn style

With so many ready-made curtains available, you don't have to sew window treatments from scratch to come up with a custom look. Instead have fun assembling new looks in natural-style colors by combining two or three ready-mades and embellishing them. Here grommets unify curtain panels of different colors and fabrics.

To make a dramatic backdrop for a bed, combine orange wide-wale corduroy panels with tie-top Indian-cotton gauze panels. Hang one pole for both, choosing one that fits through the grommets of the orange panels. Then tie the cotton panels between the corduroy curtains.

Dressed up in pretty autumn fabrics, bifold doors do a good job of adding drama to a room as they control the flow of natural light. Start with a pair of unfinished wood bifold doors bought at a lumberyard or home center store. Good fabric candidates have some stretch in them. Purchase enough fabric to wrap around each door singly. Total the size and number of doors and add 8 inches horizontally and 8 inches vertically to the width and height of each panel. Purchase the same amount of polyester quilt batting to sandwich between the fabric and the door. Remove the hinges from the doors; set them aside. Roughly cut the batting to wrap around a single panel (allow a 4-inch overlap on all sides). To fasten the batting, begin at the center of a long side, stapling it to the back side of the door. Gently stretch the batting to the corner; staple. Repeat at the opposite corner, and fill in the length with staples. Go to the opposite long side and repeat the process. Repeat at the top and bottom, turning in the batting "hospital-style" at the corners. Repeat the process for the fabric overlay; refasten hinges to the door.

autumn style **soft sided bifolds**

This is a project for two, so ask a friend to help. To stretch padding and fabric around the wooden

panels, use a staple gun from the hardware section of a lumber store or home center. One of you will

hold the fabric taut while the other fastens the fabric to the wood with the staple gun.

You can purchase sari tab curtains from shops that specialize in East Indian rugs, tapestries, and fabrics. Or, you can add tabs to sari scarves or lengths of sari fabrics that are available in specialty fabric stores, global crafts and import shops, or street markets.

who's sari now?

autumn style

The best window treatments allow light to spill through them into the room. For warm autumn light year-round, fill a window with a sheer orange or gold panel flanked by solid coordinating sheers. If you're feeling fanciful, pin a pretty printed silk scarf over the center of the warm-colored panel.

For a more dramatic window treatment, hang ready-made silk and sheer panels from ceiling to floor. Hang the curtain rod close to the ceiling on brackets attached to the wall.

Then add to the effect by decorating with pillows and throws that coordinate with the window treatment.

winter style **winter whites**

If you love the look of a landscape

freshly dusted with a blanket of snow,

bring the same clean feeling inside

with white Indian-cotton tab-top

ready-made curtain panels swept up

at the corners.

The winter-white look provides lots of natural light but may need help when it comes to providing privacy. To create a winter-white look at a window where you need privacy, purchase a rice-paper shade (import stores carry them) and enough ready-made white cotton tab-top panels to get the desired fullness. A total fabric width that measures one and a half times the width of the window is recommended.

First, hang the rice-paper shade in a permanently closed position using the screw hooks and instructions that come with the shade. Then hang a white curtain rod on white brackets just above the window frame. Slip the curtain panels onto the rod and arrange them on each side, leaving a section of the rice-paper shade revealed at the center. Finally, sew a loop at the inside bottom corner of each cotton panel. Hook the loop of each panel on the shade screw hook above it to hold the fabric in a graceful drape.

Even French doors benefit from a bit of glamour. To dress French doors with elegant stationary side panels, purchase two finished velvet panels one and a half times the width of the doors, about 24 plastic rings, and rattail cording that measures five times the fabric width. Stitch plastic rings to the backs of the panels ⅝ inch from the top and 8 inches apart. Thread the rattail cording through a ring and loop it over the rod, leaving a distance of 8 inches of cording between the rod and the curtain. Continue the threading process, positioning the cording on the rod in a zigzag arrangement.

Plain panels of velvet dress these French doors in sleek simplicity. The curtain rod is 8 inches longer than the width of the doors and is mounted on the ceiling about 24 inches from the wall. Place the panels on the rod in stationary positions spaced widely to allow access to the doors.

simply velvet *winter style*

winter style **northern lights**

For a special lighting effect, drape a string of miniature holiday lights over the curtain rod. Treat the lightbulbs to decorative reflective discs you can buy in the holiday lighting section of home center stores, or cover them with plastic hoods from shops that specialize in party lights.

Deck your halls—and your bedroom—all year, northern-lights style. For this 36- to 40-inch-wide window treatment, you need two white ready-made tab-top curtains with long tie-on straps (adjust the number of panels for wider windows, adding enough panels so the total width of the curtains is one and a half times the width of the window). For the curtain rod, purchase a ½-inch-diameter threaded rod (length should be 4 inches longer than the width of the window) at a hardware store. For finials, purchase the corresponding nuts to go with the threaded rod. You'll also need four screw eyes and very fine florist's wire. Tie the curtain straps onto the threaded rod, skipping the second one from the outer edge and the third one in from the inner edge on each panel (see detail, *above*). To hang, measure and mark four hanging points 6 inches out from the wall and equally spaced 6 inches apart. Insert the four screw eyes into the ceiling at the marks. Hand-stitch the ends of the straps together to form loops (be sure they're equal in length). Loop short lengths of florist's wire through the fabric loops and screw eyes; twist wire ends together securely and hide them behind the straps.

A wall of sheers frosts a window all year no matter what the temperature outside. Depending on the width of your window, purchase enough sheer curtain panels to equal one and a half times the width of the window. For a frosted look, purchase panels long enough to hang from ceiling to floor.

Following the instructions that come with the cable package, hang the cable "curtain rod." Depending on the type of cable you buy, you will hang the mechanism for tensing the cable on the wall or ceiling. Be sure to slip the hanging clips on the cable before locking it into the mechanism.

Fasten the sheers to the clips at 6-inch intervals.

Cables hung with tension between two points on the wall or ceiling make great barely there curtain rods, though they're suitable only for lightweight curtain panels. Purchase cables with hanging instructions from lighting supply stores or from furniture stores.

cabled sheers winter style

winter style **doubly framed**

After you've stretched a decorative fabric panel on its frame, trim it with narrow strips of wood lathe. You'll need a saw, a miter box, and small nails. If you lack woodworking skills, take your stretched fabric panels to a frame store.

For high-contrast window drama, frame each side of a blind-covered window with an arty panel made from by-the-yard fabric stretched over wood frames.

For the height of each frame, measure from the top of the window to the top of the base molding on the wall below. Or, if your fabric has a distinctive pattern to follow, adjust the size to fit the fabric pattern. For the width of each frame, follow the width suggested by the fabric's design.

Make wood frames from 1×3 lumber, mitering the corners and assembling them with corrugated fasteners. To stretch the fabric panels, ask a friend to help. Center the fabric design on the frame. Working outward from the center of one long side, staple the fabric to the edge of the frame. Gently stretch the fabric to the corner, checking for straightness; staple. Repeat at the opposite corner. Then fill in the length with staples. Go to the opposite long side and repeat the process, continually checking for straightness. Repeat at the top and bottom, turning the fabric "hospital-style" at the corners.

The ideal winter-style window is unadorned to reveal the natural view. If you need to filter strong light, however, look to ready-made sheers. You can find many in lovely winter-white hues. This window was dressed first with basic sheers, then overlaid with a delicate spangled fashion scarf.

First, hang plain, ready-made sheers in the window on tension rods. Then, using large clips from an office-supply store, fasten the ends of a fashion scarf over the plain panel onto the rod.

If you like the idea of dressing up basic sheers with a sparkly fashion scarf, you'll find what you need in upscale fashion-accessory stores. Look for a lightweight off-white organza scarf edged in silver thread, fringed generously, or dusted with glittering rhinestones or tiny mirrors.

it's in the clip winter style

bringing your **natural style** home

style profile

For **WINDOW TREATMENTS** that soften the architecture and filter light without blocking it, check **Pottery Barn's** embroidered sheer organdy or nubby linen draperies. For a catalog, call **800/922-5507,** or visit the website at **potterybarn.com. Restoration Hardware** is another accessible source, featuring sheer, opaque, and subtly textured Belgian linen draperies, as well as breezy silk organzas. Call **800/762-1005** for a catalog or visit the website at **restorationhardware.com.**

D-I-Y ROOM DIVIDERS, such as those shown on pages 10 and 12, can be made by stapling vintage fabric or a bamboo window blind on an artist's stretcher frame. Natural blinds from **CostPlus World Market** are available nationwide. To locate vintage fabrics for stretching on the frame, check estate sales, antiques shops, and antiques fairs, as well as online auctions such as **ebay** and **Yahoo Auctions.**

FURNITURE and RUGS shown on pages 8–14 are from **IKEA's mail-order catalog.** Call **800/434-4532** to locate the store nearest you or to order a current catalog. Online: **ikea.com.** For paper globe lamps, visit a **Pier 1 Imports.**. Log on to **Pier 1.com** for store location nearest you. Pier 1 is also a reliable source for **WOVEN BASKETS** in a variety of fibers, ethnic designs, and sizes ranging from laundry hampers to bread baskets. The tulip fabric (Tulip Trance #665922) used to upholster the chair on page 8 is from **Waverly.** If the fabric isn't available in a store near you, call consumer information at **800/423-5881** for help in finding it or a substitute (fabrics may be discontinued without notice). For more information on Waverly fabrics, visit the website at **waverly.com.**

spring style

In Venice, Florida, just a half hour's drive south of Sarasota, **The Cat's Meow** offers everything you need for fresh and inviting **SPRING-STYLE COMFORT.** Located at 235 West Miami Avenue, the shop's enchanting spaces offer Shabby Chic fabrics, sofas, chairs, and ottomans; unusual vintage wicker and chandeliers; painted tables, handcrafted accessories and jewelry; and tableware. You'll also find a lavish bed, bath, and candle selection. For information, call **941/486-1650** or send an e-mail to **Shabby.Susie@verizon.net.**

Especially Lace (202 Fifth Street, West Des Moines, IA 50265) sells **ANTIQUE and NEW LACE** curtains and linens as well as selected items from the April Cornell line and products from Jardin du Soleil, Crabtree & Evelyn, The Good Home, and more. Worth a visit in person or on the web at **especiallylace.com.** For ideas to create outdoor rooms, visit **bhg.com/bkfreshair.** To craft comfortable spaces indoors and out, visit **bhg.com/bkhousehome.**

Natural light is optimal for getting that spring-style feeling, but those who depend on artifical light in their homes can take comfort in today's range of **INTERIOR LIGHTING OPTIONS,** which, when thoughtfully varied, can approximate the day's changing lights. Incandescent tungsten bulbs emit a yellowish light and are best used during the morning hours in bedrooms, baths, and breakfast nooks, where they evoke the golden glow of a southern exposure. Full-spectrum bulbs are the closest replication of natural light available, emitting the same balance of colors as overhead sunlight while reducing glare and eyestrain. Useful as task lighting replacing the murky dull white of overhead lighting in kitchens, dressing rooms, or home offices, full-spectrum bulbs are also available in the form of light boxes. These portable boxes are used to alleviate symptoms associated with the winter doldrums (seasonal affective disorder), jet lag, fatigue, and insomnia. Halogen lights are also good for capturing true color and replicating the even white illumination of a northern exposure. Use low-voltage halogen lighting to illuminate art, or install halogen bulbs in a crafts room or studio. At night, choose shaded lamps, uplights such as sconces and chandeliers, or moody wall washers instead of harsh overhead lighting. Avoid traditional fluorescent lighting, which can increase irritability and fatigue. For more information on **DESIGNING A HOUSEHOLD LIGHTING PLAN,** and for links to retail showrooms, visit the Consumer Resources page of the website of the **American Lighting Association** at **americanlightingassoc.com.**

Sculpt space and create inviting ambience with light using **DIMMER SWITCHES.** If you don't want to spend time replacing wall switches with dimmers, use lamp dimmers. Simply plug a table lamp into the dimmer and plug the dimmer cord into the wall. Look for dimmers at home improvement centers and lighting stores.

For **PILLOW COVERS, QUILTS, COVERLETS, and SHEETS** in Provençal-inspired cottons, and embroidered sheers in spring color themes, visit **April Cornell,** a retail chain. To find a store near you, visit the website at **aprilcornell.com.**

summer style

For furniture that works both inside and out, check catalogs, stores, and websites based on **OUTDOOR LIVING**. **Smith & Hawken's** catalog offers outdoor furniture, lanterns, fire pits, and hammocks to use on patios and decks, in gardens and sunrooms. For summer style inside your home, consider using garden benches and chairs around a dining table or a single piece as a garden accent in a bedroom. Call **800/940-1170** to request a catalog or visit the web store at **SmithandHawken.com.**

The **COOLEST SHEETS** on the market today are made from 100 percent Egyptian cotton or American pima cotton (labeled with the trademark "Supima"). Knowing the type of cotton is often a better indicator of quality than thread count. For feel-good bedding in beautiful colors and patterns, buy online or by catalog from some of the best-known companies: **Garnet Hill (garnethill.com), The Company Store (thecompanystore.com),** and **Land's End (landsend.com)**. Land's End sells oxford-cloth sheets that feel like your favorite shirt; also shop here for summer-style waffle-weave towels. **Chambers** sells exquisite high-end imported bedding and towels. Call **800/334-9790** for a catalog. Shopping pros recommend watching for their sales.

For splash-in-the-bath **WATERWORKS**, check out the new showerhead from **Moen.** Its patented Revolution massaging showerhead sends out a spiral of water that can be dialed up for deep massage or down to a rainlike shower. It's available for about $60 at **Lowe's, Target, Bed Bath and Beyond,** plumbing showrooms, and online at the company's website **moen.com.** The fixture isn't considered low-flow, but all showerheads are limited by federal regulation to 5.5 gallons per minute (old showerheads could use as much as 8 gallons per minute), and it isn't affected by low water pressure. For more information, visit the website. The Nature S Curve showerhead ($40) by **AquatekInternational** drenches you with even pressure from every point on the 5½-inch-diameter head. Call **800/640-4139** or visit the website, **aquatekinternational.com.** To install these and most other showerheads onto standard water pipes, remove the old fixture and clean the pipe threads. Wrap the shower arm with Teflon for a secure seal, then screw on the new showerhead.

Check the **Crate & Barrel** summer catalogs each year for **CASUAL TABLEWARE** and **OUTDOOR FURNITURE** that's beautiful enough to use inside the house all year-round. The furniture styles are often drawn from year-round Caribbean island-style living and manufactured with natural materials such as cane and rattan. For the store nearest you, call **800/996-9960.** To place a quick catalog order, visit **crateandbarrel.com.** For European bistro-style dining in your kitchen,

shop **Ballard Design's** catalog. You'll find metal sidewalk seating and tables as well as cane and bamboo folding chairs that can be painted with brilliant indoor-outdoor paints. Shop online at **ballarddesigns.com** or call **800/367-2810** to request a catalog. Visit Ballard outlet centers near Atlanta (1670 DeFoor Avenue, 404/603-7033) or Cincinnati (8939 Union Centre Boulevard, 513/603-1333) to save on samples, overstocks, and discontinued items.

autumn style

For **CLASSIC FURNITURE** made with enduring style and built from wood and natural steel, shop **Room & Board**, a Minneapolis-based home furnishings store at 4600 Olson Memorial Highway. You can call **800/486-6554** for store locations in California, Colorado, and Illinois or visit online at **room&board.com.** Out of respect for the environment, the annual catalog is mailed once a year. Copies are available in stores and upon request at the website.

Vintage, a Des Moines-based company, creates whimsical assemblage sculptures, mirrors, and **TIN-CEILING CONTAINERS** such as the one shown on page 119. For information, call **515/981-5189** or check out the website at **vintagesculpture.com**.

Pottery Barn offers affordable chenille thows, pillows, **SINK-IN SEATING**, and ottomans for your feet. For a catalog, call **800/922-5507** or visit the website at **potterybarn.com. Restoration Hardware's** comfortable sectional sofas, Italian leather chairs, peasant-style trestle-legged tables, and upholstered dining chairs make autumn-style living and dining easy to achieve. Visit the stores (call **800/762-1005** for the store location nearest you), shop the catalog, or check the website at **restorationhardware.com.**

ABC Carpet & Home in New York City **(212/473-3000)** and Delray Beach, Florida **(561/279-7777),** well known for quality **HANDWOVEN ORIENTAL CARPETS,** is also a large retailer of extra-luxury bedding, including soft wool and cashmere blankets, fluffy down pillows and comforters, natural cotton matelassé coverlets, regal Italian damask sheets, and silk charmeuse duvet covers. Visit online at **abccarpet.com.**

Sobagara (sobagara.com) is a quality supplier of **BUCKWHEAT HULL PILLOWS.** The stuffing, composed of the outside part of the buckwheat seed milled off before grinding, is hypoallergenic and long-lasting. It conforms to your body as you move, dissipating heat so you can stay warm in winter and cool in summer. In addition to standard pillows, Sobagara offers baby pillows, travel pillows, and body pillows.

HEATED TOWEL RACKS can be ordered from **Warmrails, Inc., 877/927-6724, warmrails.com; Comfort House, comforthouse.com; Chambers, 800/334-9790;** and **Hammacher Schlemmer, 800/543-3366.**

If you're serious about **GETTING ORGANIZED** and decluttering your life, visit **bhg.com/bkorganize** for lots of tips and practical ideas. To contain everything you organize, turn the pages of **Hold Everything's** current catalog. (Call **800/421-2285** to request a catalog.) Then choose from classic shelving, furniture, and accessories to put everything in place.

winter style

For **ELECTRIC FIREPLACES**, check out these two companies: **Dimplex** at **dimplex.com** or **Heat-N-Glo**, a division of **Hearth Technologies**, at **heatnglo.com.** Scroll through their mantel and grill choices, too.

For **REMOTE-CONTROL LIGHTING** that covers your whole house, look into **Lutron's RadioRa** whole-house lighting control system. It uses a regulated radio frequency that isn't affected by power lines, cordless phones, or other wireless products and gives you one-touch control of any light or group of lights in the house. Installing the system involves replacing standard light switches with RadioRa dimmers and switches and plugging lamps into table-lamp controls. Installation and setup must be done by an electrician, who also can link the controls to your home security system and a RadioRa car-visor control that lets you turn lights on and off from the car. The cost of installation averages $200 to $300 per location in your home—so equipping the entry and the master bedroom, for example, would run between $400 and $600. For more information, visit the website at **lutron.com/radiora** or call the Lutron Hotline, **800/523-9466.**

Design Within Reach stocks the best of **MODERN-DESIGN FURNITURE** and is ready to ship. Affordable prices on clean-lined, winter-style home furnishings make this a fast-growing company. See their products online at **dwr.com,** or order from their catalog. **Topdeq** offers European-designed office furnishings. Call **866/876-3300** to request a catalog or view products online at **topdeq.com**. A delightful source for witty modern furnishings: **Living Walls,** located at 1311 Main Street, Sarasota, Florida **(941/957-4411).** Check out the website at **livingwalls.com.**

In New York City, visit the Museum of Modern Art's design stores for **INNOVATIVE HOME ACCESSORIES.** Choose from two locations: one at 44 West 53 Street, another in SoHo at 81 Spring Street. The Museum Store location: 33 Street at Queens Boulevard, Long Island City, N.Y. To order from the catalog or to request one, call **800/447-6662**. Visit the website at **momastore.org.**

CANDLES are available at discount stores and superstores, but know that when it comes to quality, you get what you pay for. Many inexpensive, chemically scented candles can burn dirty and emit toxins into the air. Handmade candles are best, scented with essential oils and made from a food-grade paraffin wax. For the best scents, check out shops that specialize in home fragrances, aromatherapy products, and bath fragrances. **Illuminations** at **Illuminations.com** offers a good selection. Another source: **Illume Candles, Inc.** Visit the website at **illumecandles.com** to see the product line; orders can be placed by phone. Call **800/245-5863** between 10 a.m. and 6 p.m. PST.

For **CANDLE SAFETY**, never leave a burning candle unattended and keep wicks trimmed to $1/8$ to $1/4$ inch. If the tip of a wick has curled to one side, it has burned too long. To approximate the burning time of a quality candle, multiply one hour times each inch of candle diameter. Candles kept in one place for a long period of time should be rotated occasionally to allow for even burning. Never let matches burn in the candle's pool of melting wax. Watch for drips from drafts, and keep burning candles away from enclosed spaces such as bookshelves. Extinguish candles that have burned down to within 2 inches of their holders.

window treatments

Smith + Noble Windoware offers a wide range of **SHADES, BLINDS, SHUTTERS, CORNICES,** and **DRAPERIES** to custom-order for your windows. The company also carries a fabric collection from which you can select fabric swatches. To order swatches, call **800/248-8888** or visit the website **(smithandnoble.com)** to select them. The $5 fee for the service is applicable toward any order over $100 placed within 90 days. Import stores, such as World Market and Pier 1, are also good sources for blinds, shades, and fabric curtain panels in natural fabrics.

Waverly fabrics for draperies and curtains are available nationally (the fabric for the curtain panel on the left of page 163 is Waverly pattern #665024).Or, visit **waverly.com** and view the company's fabrics. Call consumer information at **800/423-5881** for help in finding a substitute fabric (fabrics may be discontinued without notice). Another excellent source for fabrics is **Calico Corners,** with stores located nationwide..

credits and contributors

research and styling assistance amy underwood

styling assistance susie holt

photography scott little pages 6 top left, 17 top right, 43, 105. 110 left, 111 bottom left, 113, 119 top left, 125 top left and right, 141, 146 left, 147, 152, 153 top left, bottom right, 155, 157, 160 left, 161 top, 162-163, 165, 170-171, 176, 178, 182, 184-187

photography william stites pages 6 top right, 10 center right and bottom right, 16 top right, 17 top left, 20, 23-27, 38 right, 39 left and right, 41 top right, 46 right, 47 bottom left and top, 52 right, 53, 54, 69, 72 right, 73 left and center, 75–77, 80 left, 86–87, 88 right, 89 bottom right, 121

photography kim cornelison pages 8, 10, 12, 14, 17 top center, 29, 30, 64–67, 80 right, 81 bottom center and right, 100–103, 118 left, 119 bottom left, 124 right, 125 bottom left, 136–139

photography allen jerdee page 15 center right

Additional photography courtesy of the following Meredith publications: *Better Homes and Gardens*® magazine, *Traditional Home*® magazine, *Better Homes and Gardens*® *Home Ideas* magazine, *Better Homes and Gardens*® *Do It Yourself* magazine, *Home Garden* magazine

special thanks to **Waverly** and **Seabrook** for providing fabrics and wallcoverings for pages 30–31, 66–67, 102–103, 138–139, and 163 left and to **The Cat's Meow,** Venice, Florida, for lending furniture and fabrics for photography on pages 21–27, 38–39, 46–47, and 52–53.

A-B

Accessories
  autumn style, 94, 110–111, 118–119, 124–125
  spring style, 22, 38–39, 46–47, 52–53
  summer style, 58, 72–73, 80–81, 88–89
  winter style, 133, 146–147, 152–153, 160–161
Artwork, 40–41, 84, 124–125, 146
Autumn style, 90–125
  accessories, 110–111, 118–119, 124–125
  bedrooms, 120–125
  color, 97, 99, 100–103, 117
  decorating basics, 93–94
  dining areas, 98–99, 112–119
  living areas, 12, 95–97, 104–111
  profile, 12–13, 17
  textures and patterns, 102–103, 108
  window treatments, 108, 176–181

Bedding, 49, 83, 155
Bedrooms
  autumn style, 120–125
  spring style, 26, 48–53
  summer style, 60–61, 82–89
  winter style, 134–135, 154–161
Bookshelves, display on, 89

C-D

Candles, 147, 152–153
Chandeliers, 27, 34–35, 89
Color
  autumn style, 97, 99–103, 117
  for linking diverse pieces, 33
  mixing styles, 44–45
  spring style, 22, 28–31
  summer style, 58, 64–67, 70
  winter style, 130, 136–139, 142, 157, 159
Curtains. See Window treatments

Dining areas
  autumn style, 98–99, 112–119
  spring style, 25, 40–45
  summer style, 62–63, 74–81
  winter style, 148–153
Dinnerware, 42, 46–47, 81, 153, 166
Draperies. See Window treatments

F

Fall style. See Autumn style
Fireplace mantel, display on, 110
Fireplaces, 134–135, 140, 141, 151
Floral arrangements
  autumn style, 111, 119
  spring style, 39, 42, 47, 52, 53
  summer style, 59–60, 72, 78–79
  winter style, 147, 161
Focal point, creation of, 109
Furniture, arrangement and shape of, 22, 58, 94, 105, 130

L-N

Light, use of, 34, 159
Lighting
  autumn style, 124–125
  spring style, 27
  summer style, 74, 76, 88–89
  winter style, 146–147, 152, 184
Living areas
  autumn style, 12, 92, 95–97, 104–111
  spring style, 8, 22, 23, 32–39
  summer style, 10, 68–73
  winter style, 14, 128, 129, 140–147

Minimalism, 57
Mirrors, 27, 58, 111
Mixing, of styles, 44–45, 106, 114–115, 117

Neutrals, 33

O-P

Occasional tables, 47, 85, 89, 110–111
Outdoor spaces, 74–75, 78, 79

Pattern
  autumn style, 102–103, 108
  mixing styles, 45
  spring style, 30–31
  summer style, 66–67
  winter style, 138–139, 142
Pictures, 40–41, 72, 84, 124, 146
Pillows, 50, 51, 53, 125, 160, 161
Plate racks, 42, 166
Porches, 20, 24–25

Q-S

Quiz, for finding natural style, 16–17

Reading alcove, 108
Red, use of, 98, 99, 158, 159

Shape, use of, 130, 159
Sleeping berth, 85
Space-enhancing ideas, 37, 58, 86, 87
Spring style, 18–53
  accessories, 22, 38–39, 46–47, 52–53
  bedrooms, 26, 48–53
  color, 22, 28–31
  decorating basics, 21–22
  dining areas, 25, 40–45
  living areas, 8, 22–23, 32–39
  profile, 8–9, 17
  textures and patterns, 30–31
  window treatments, 164–169
Style quiz, 16–17
Summer style, 54–89
  accessories, 58, 72–73, 80–81, 88–89
  bedrooms, 60–61, 82–89
  color, 58, 64–67, 70

decorating basics, 57–58
dining areas, 62–63, 74–81
living areas, 10, 68–73
mixing with autumn style, 114–115
profile, 10–11, 17
textures and patterns, 66–67
window treatments, 170–175
Sunrooms, 34–35

T-W

Tables, dining. See Dining areas
Tables, occasional, 47, 88–89, 110–111
Test, for finding natural style, 16–17
Texture
  autumn style, 102–103
  mixing styles, 45
  spring style, 30–31
  summer style, 66–67
  winter style, 138–139

Wall hangings, 40–41, 72, 84, 124–125, 146–147
White, use of
  spring style, 22
  summer style, 58, 86
  winter style, 136, 157, 159
Window treatments, 162–187
  autumn style, 176–181
  spring style, 164–169
  summer style, 170–175
  winter style, 130, 182–187
Winter style, 126–161
  accessories, 133, 146–147, 152–153, 160–161
  bedrooms, 134–135, 154–161
  color, 130, 136–139, 142, 157, 159
  decorating basics, 129–130
  dining areas, 148–153
  living areas, 14, 128, 129, 140–147
  profile, 14–15, 17
  textures and patterns, 138–139, 142
  window treatments, 130, 182–187